# Mothers

### of the

# Wise

### and

# Good

*Her children arise up and call her blessed.*
*—Proverbs 31:28*

## Jabez Burns

SOLID GROUND

SOLID GROUND CHRISTIAN BOOKS
Box 660132, Vestavia Hills, AL 35266

*Mothers of the Wise and Good*
*by Jabez Burns*
Published by Solid Ground Christian Books
© 2001, Solid Ground Christian Books
All Rights Reserved

Cover: Anthony Rotolo Design


Manufactured in the United States of America
1  2  3  4  5  6  7  8  9  10     01  02  03  04  05

# Preface

Mothers of the Wise and Good *has been selected to be the first book published by Solid Ground Christian Books. It is believed that it will accomplish in the twenty-first century what it did in the nineteenth when it was first written.*

*Jabez Burns was a pastor who understood the role and value of mothers. He knew from personal experience the power of a godly mother (see pp. 184-188), and he was passionate about his concern that his generation would value and cherish the high calling of motherhood.*

*Our day is reaping what it has sown for many years. It has been nearly two generations that have sown the seeds of radical feminism, and we have been reaping the bitter and ugly fruits in our day. It is our desire that the Lord will use a book like this to restore to women a proper view of their highest calling, the calling of motherhood. Hear now the words of Jabez Burns as he wrote the preface to this volume when it first appeared in March 1846...*

I t is evident that the first and deepest impressions are made on the minds of children by mothers. It is under their maternal attention that the physical form is gently reared, the intellectual faculties elicited, and the moral powers fostered and directed. To discharge this threefold office, what knowledge, skill, kindness, fidelity, and perseverance are requisite! How important that the earliest lessons and impressions should be those of wisdom, goodness, and piety; and not of folly, ignorance, and irreligion! As is the mother, extensively and generally, so will be the children. The child will, and must, from the very necessity of things, be powerfully influenced by the maternal character which presides over it.

It is a rare thing to meet with a dull and ignorant child who has had the fostering care of an intelligent mother; so that the province she occupies is one of the most important and momentous, to the interests of mind, in which a responsible being can possibly be placed.

Now, it is of the highest import that mothers should be awakened and duly instructed as to this responsibility itself. A deep sense of these moral obligations would lead to an earnest desire to know by what means the onerous duties could best be discharged. Instruction would be diligently sought, examples would be eagerly contemplated, and Divine aid would be fervently implored.

The writer has been powerfully struck by the fact, that there are few good works which are directly adapted to give the information, and supply the help which is needed. Good thoughts and interesting facts on this subject are scattered abroad through the length and breadth of our moral and religious literature; but thus it is almost unavailable to those whose benefit and encouragement should be chiefly aimed at.

The plan designed in this volume has been to furnish within a portable and convenient size, a series of delightful instances of the success of pious maternal influence, interspersed with various striking incidents, both in prose and verse, calculated to interest and improve the mind, and followed by short essays on the various duties and responsibilities of the Christian mother.

To collect and arrange has been the chief duty of the Author, being satisfied that it would have been impossible, for him, at least, to have provided original articles of equal value, and as directly adapted to the end contemplated. That the book may prove instructive, edifying, and useful, under God's blessing, to that most numerous, important, and influential class for whom it has been chiefly designed, is the earnest and prayerful desire of the Author.

# CONTENTS.

1*

STRIKING INCIDENTS AND BRIEF ACCOUNTS OF
DISTINGUISHED MOTHERS, &c.

# MOTHERS OF THE WISE AND GOOD.

## INTRODUCTORY CHAPTER.

THE most tender interests and the most ardent hopes, both of individuals and society, ever rest fondly and anxiously upon the young ; consequently the influences that minister to the growth of moral and mental excellence, in the youthful mind, must be one of the most important topics on which the reflective and conscientious inquirer can dwell. Common observation, as well as careful investigation, have long decided, that the maternal influence is all-powerful in forming the habits and developing the faculties, at that important period of life, when the opening mind is like wax to receive an impression, and like marble to retain it. The fact is incontrovertible, that the impressions which linger with the greatest tenacity in the memory, are those which were traced the earliest ; hence it follows, that the office of mother is not only the most dear and interesting, but the most important and responsible that can devolve on woman.

The influence of mothers is of a kind that the institutions of society, in different ages of the world, cannot materially affect or deteriorate. Thus, even in nations and times when women were depressed by all the cruelty and tyranny of heathen institutions, maternal influence still operated powerfully; and the annals of classic antiquity show us that heathen Greece and Rome boasted of mothers who nobly trained their sons to the service of their country—who incited the studious to aspire to the dignities of the senator, and the ardent to pursue the fierce and stern triumph of the warrior.    Ambition—an ambition created by false systems of faith, seems to have been the leading motive that prompted all the devotedness which the matrons of heathen antiquity displayed : but happily, under our pure and hallowed faith, the Christian mother's holy office, is not to teach stern contempt of pain, reckless love of danger, fierce hatred of enemies, and all the wild catalogue of harsh attainments, once falsely thought necessary to form an heroic character; but hers is the nobler and more congenial task to implant in the fresh soil of the youthful mind, the seeds of all the gentler moral virtues, and all the lovely Christian graces.

The mother who desires to be qualified for her high and onerous office, must first be taught of Him who is the fountain of all knowledge.   If her soul be illumined with wisdom from on high, and her mind be adorned with the beauty of holiness, then is she qualified to become, in the best sense of the term, the moral guide and teacher of her offspring;—and wherever children gain their merely intellectual culture, it is always best for them, that they obtain their first knowledge of religious truths and moral duties, from the teachings of a mother. Natural tenderness in this case comes to aid both the teacher and the taught, the lesson is given and received in love; it is written not only on the mind, but it sinks deep into the heart and dwells there, unerased through long years, influencing the feelings, regulating and purifying the impulses; and its effect, like bread cast upon the waters, is found after many days.

To dwell on the solemn responsibility of the maternal office, might have the tendency to depress the humble and the diffident. The anxious mother, thinking of the immortal mind consigned to her care and teaching,—beholding a creature to be trained for time and eternity, may indeed often be constrained to exclaim: "Who is sufficient for these things?" Unwise indeed would be that mother, who was confident only in the strength of feeble, erring human nature, for the qualifications of her high office; but if, in humble, prayerful dependence on the Divine blessing, she enters on the work of the education of her offspring, the probabilities are all in favor of her realizing, in the success of her sincere endeavors, an exceeding great reward. The cases are very rare where a judicious, tender, persevering mother has been disappointed by the objects of her solicitude. It is scarcely in human nature, degraded as it is, to resist the influence of example—the pleadings of tenderness, the admonitions of reason, from a mother who " openeth her mouth with wisdom, and in her tongue is the law of kindness."

But admit that in some very rare instances a painful, rather than a pleasing result, has followed a wise and faithful discharge of maternal duty. Yet the good and pious mother, in her distress, is not without that consolation which follows on the right fulfillment of a trust. No self-accusation, no remorse mingles bitterness with her sorrows,—and while life remains to her erring child, the hope by her is fondly and rationally cherished, that the good seed sown is latent, not lost; and that though apparently sterile the soil, ultimately it will germinate, and produce fruits of repentance and amendment.

Facts are the best illustrations of argument, and happily the biography of the wise and good in every age furnishes materials full of encouragement for the timid —of comfort for the anxious—of hope for the disappointed, and of instruction for all who bear the sacred name of mother.

The plans of early training, that have resulted in eminent success; the qualifications requisite to the right performance of duty; the trials that have at length had a happy issue; are all more impressive from the details of actual practical experience, than in theoretical disquisitions.

There is no subject on which theory and practice have been more opposed to each other, than on that of education. Almost every intelligent mother has found that difficulties occurred in her daily task, which no theoretic writer could fully anticipate; details involving important results, which were too minute for the essayist to enter into, and trials which no system could exactly meet or obviate; then, when arguments seemed inapplicable and tedious, an anecdote of real life has stimulated flagging energies, kindled fresh hopes, animated to continued exertion, and sustained to that perseverance, in well-doing, which has the blessed promise, " In due time ye shall reap, if ye faint not."

If the lives of great and good men be one of the most improving studies that can engage the attention of the inquiring mind; of equal value must be the detail, however slight, that is given of the maternal influence under which those great men were trained: of the moral and mental nurture which aided in developing the mind, and forming the habits. And when it is proved that home influences, the gentle wisdom of the maternal mind, the devoted tenderness of the maternal heart, have been more mighty for good than any other influence—the example and inference must be most cheering and encouraging to those who are engaged in the fulfillment of similar duties. To such the following anecdotes of the mothers of some of the wisest and best of human beings, cannot fail to be peculiarly interesting and instructive, since they possess all the advantage which practice has over theory, example over precept. Take courage, therefore, oh! pious, tender mother; many of the mothers of earth's mightiest have, as thou wilt see, sown precious seed weeping, but come again rejoicing, bearing their sheaves with them.

2

## MONICA AND ST. AUGUSTINE.

THIS venerable man was born in the city of Tagasta, in Numidia. His father, Patricius, continued a Pagan till near his death; when, won by the amiable conversation of his wife, he died in the Christian faith. His mother, Monica, eminent for piety, endeavored early to instil into his infant mind the pure doctrines of Divine truth, recommending what she taught by her holy life. But that God, without the influence of whose Spirit all teaching is ineffectual, is sometimes pleased to exercise the faith and patience of his people, that they may "Be still, and know that he is God;" and ascribe, not to themselves, but to His name, all the glory. Augustine, at an early age, became acquainted with men, who, led away by false learning, were ignorant of the true God. Oh, how dangerous is the snare of evil friendship! It is the nature of sin to deceive, by the false shadow of that good, which in God alone is to be found; and He only who formed the heart, can raise it from the low and groveling objects, in pursuit of which, every man in his own ways will wander, to behold the glory and excellency of Him in whose presence there is "fullness of joy."

Augustine was early instructed in the Greek and Latin languages, in which he made very great progress. "Who did not extol," says he, "the noble spirit of my father, in laying out so much money, in the education of his son, while yet he had no concern in what manner I grew up to Thee?" Eloquent, learned, and esteemed wise, Augustine was yet ignorant of that God, who, though his throne is in the highest heaven, dwells also in the humble and contrite heart. "My pride," he says, "separated me from Thee, and closed my eyes. I am willing to recollect the scenes of base- ness through which I have passed: not, that I may love them, but love Thee, my God. I do it from the love of Thy love, recollecting my own very evil ways, in the bitterness of memory, that Thou mayest be en- deared to me. My soul is a habitation too narrow for Thy entrance; do Thou enlarge it; it is in ruins, do Thou repair it: it has what must offend thine eyes, who shall cleanse it, or to whom shall I cry, but unto Thee? Still, O Lord, in my childhood, I have much to praise Thee for; for many—many were thy gifts. The sin was mine that I sought pleasure, truth, and happiness, not in Thee, but in the creature, and thus rushed into pains, confusion, and errors. While I was yet walking in sin, often attempting to rise, and sink- ing still deeper, my dear mother, in vigorous hope, persisted in earnest prayer for me. I remember also, that she entreated a certain bishop to undertake to reason me out of my errors. "Your son," says he, "is too much elated at present, and carried away with the pleasing novelties of his opinion, to regard any argument. Let him alone, only continue praying to the Lord for him; in the course of his study he will discover his error." All this satisfied not my anxious parent; with floods of tears she still per-

sisted in her request, till a little out of patience,
with her importunity, he said, "Begone, good woman,
it is impossible that the child of such tears should
perish."

While I was teaching rhetoric in my native town, I
enjoyed the friendship of a young man of my own
age; it was a regard influenced by similar studies.
He was soon afterward seized with a fever.   I, who
loved him with much tenderness, came, not to speak
of that Saviour, the knowledge of whose name only,
can make the dying sinner triumph over his last and
dreadful enemy, but to converse on the subjects in
which we were wont to rejoice.   That vain philosophy
could not soothe his dying ear.   Delivered from my
madness, he was saved by thee, O God!  After the
death of my friend, I was indeed wretched; and
wretched is every soul that is bound by the love of
mortal things.   The load of misery burdened me: I
knew Thou alone couldst care; but I was unwilling,
weak and helpless.   Thy hand, my God, in the secret
of thy providence, forsook not my soul; day and
night the prayers of my mother came up before Thee,
and thou wroughtest on me, in a way marvelous indeed.  I was now, in my thirtieth year, still miserable.
Troubled in my conscience to set apart some portion
of my time each day for the care of my soul, but then,
what time shall I have to attend the levees of the great,
for study, and for relaxation?   What then, if death
should suddenly seize you, and judgment overtake you
unprepared?   Men's goings are from the Lord; it was

from thy influence that I was persuaded to go to Rome
instead of Carthage.   The deep recesses of Thy wisdom must be confessed by me in this dispensation.
The true cause of this removal was hidden, at this
time, from me and my mother, who bewailed at my
going away, and followed me to the sea-side.   I deceived her, though she held me close, with a view to
hold me backward, or go along with me.   I pretended
that I meant only to stay with a friend until he should
sail.   That night I departed privily, and she remained,
weeping and praying.   Thus did I deceive her who
was such a mother to me !   Yet was I preserved from
the dangers of the sea ; and there was a time coming,
when Thou wouldst wipe away my mother's tears, with
which she watered the earth, and forgive this my base
undutifulness.   Courageous through piety, and following me through sea and land, she at length found me
still hopeless with respect to the discovery of divine
truth. Ambrose, the pious bishop of Milan, was charmed
with the fervency of her piety, and the amiableness of
her good works.   I was delighted with his learning, and
the sweetness of his language.   I sought for opportunities of conversing with him ; but engaged in study,
and surrounded at all times by persons whose necessi-
ties he relieved, I sought in vain.   His sermons, however, were profitable to me.   Let the Christian orator
pray before he speak.   Let him lift up his thirsty soul
to God, before he pronounce anything.   Ambrose had
thus prayed for me.   The state of my mind was now
altered : my meditations on Thee, my God, were like

the attempts of men, desirous of awaking, but sinking
again into sleep.  But Thou, with whom are the hearts
of all, didst shine on me vehemently; I trembled; I
now sought the way of obtaining strength to enjoy
Thee, and found it not till I embraced, " the Media-
tor between God and man,—the man Christ Jesus,"
who is " God over all blessed for ever," calling and
saying, " I am the way, the truth, and the life."  With
eagerness I took up the volume of inspiration, particularly the writings of St. Paul.  Here now appeared
one uniform tenor of godliness, and I learned to rejoice
with trembling.  The books in which I delighted, had
none of the blessed realities which I found here, namely, Salvation, the Holy Spirit, and the Cup of Redemption.  In the others, no one hears, " Come unto me all
ye that are weary and heavy laden, and I will give you
rest."  I determined to return to Africa with my mother: and while preparations were made for our departure, we stood in a window facing the coast, at the
mouth of the Tiber.  We conversed on the eternal
life of the saints.  It was evident to us, that earthly
pleasures deserved not to be named in comparison.
Erecting our spirits most ardently, we ascended above
the noblest parts of material creation to Thee, by whom
all things were made.  In that moment the world appeared to us of no value, and she said soon, " What do
I here?  One thing only—your conversion—was an
object for which I wished to live.  My God has given
me this in larger measure: what do I here?"  Five
days afterward she fell into a fever, of which she died.

One who was with us lamented that she was likely to leave her body in a foreign land : she looked with anxiety to see his conception so groveling. " Place this body anywhere ; do not distress yourself about it. Nothing," said she, "·is far to God,—I don't fear that he should know where to find it at the resurrection !"

Soon after the loss of his inestimable parent, Augustine returned into Africa ; where, by his preaching, divine truth, which had almost been buried amidst many errors, raised again its head.   His writings were translated into the Greek tongue, and diffused with vigor through the Christian world.   For more than a thousand years previous to the Reformation, the light of divine truth, which shone here and there among individuals, during the dreary night of superstition, was, in many instances, kindled, preserved, and increased by his writings, which, next to the Holy Scriptures, were the guides of men who feared God : nor have we in all history, an instance of so extensive utility derived to the church by the works of men.   Still they are read with delight and edification by thousands.   Augustine, jealous of the honor of the Divine word, contended zealously " for the faith once delivered to the saints," but was in every controversy distinguished by a spirit of meekness and humility, remembering that " the wrath of man worketh not the righteousness of God ;" and that the servants of the Lord must not strive, but be " gentle unto all, apt to teach, patient." Moderate in his dress, furniture and diet, he constantly practiced hospitality.   As one evidence of his humble,

2*

tender, watchful spirit, he had it written on his table, that, whoever attacked the characters of the absent, should be excluded.   On one occasion, some bishops with whom he was intimate, breaking the rule, he was at length so much roused as to say, that either those lines must be erased from his table, or he would retire to his chamber.   He was very attentive to the wants and comforts of the poor.   His sermons were plain, weighty, serious and affectionate.   He followed his own rules, and was himself the preacher he described. At length, this venerable servant of God was seized with a fever, which ended in his dissolution in the year 430.   He lived seventy-six years; forty of which he had been a presbyter or bishop.   He used to say, that "a Christian should never cease to repent till the hour of his death."   He had David's penitential psalms inscribed on his wall during his last illness.   For more than fourteen hundred years, Augustine has doubtless been in heaven, blessing and adoring God for his pious mother; and "though dead he yet speaketh" to all Christian parents, to spare no pains for the conversion of their children, assured that they "who sow in tears shall reap in joy."

## THE MOTHER OF KING ALFRED THE GREAT.

THE name of Alfred the Great, though not the earliest, was undoubtedly the most eminent that dignifies our legislative and regal annals.   Beloved by his father far above his other sons, every indulgence that could have enervated a less noble mind, was shown him.   When a mere child, his health being delicate, he was sent with a princely retinue to travel in the South of Europe, and twice before he had attained his ninth year, he had accompanied his royal parent to Rome, then the great resort of all that was learned and wise in the civilized world.   But with advantages thus early bestowed, unusual alike to his tender age and the time in which he flourished, and with expenditure profusely lavished upon him, yet so unenlightened was the period in which he lived, that Alfred at twelve years of age could neither read nor write.

The development of those rare intellectual qualities which surmounted every obstacle which desultory habits may be supposed to have induced, when confirmed by rank, wealth, and the absence of all control, was mainly attributable to his step-mother, Judith, the queen of Ethelwulf.   She was a princess of great learning and rare accomplishments for that early period; and having promised a finely illuminated book of Saxon poems—to which Alfred had been listening with enthusiasm—to such of her sons as should the soonest be able to read them, the innate energy of

Alfred's dormant talents were roused, and the foundation was laid of that learning which produced the greatest benefit to his country.

It is said, that when this promise of the book was made, "Alfred returning to Queen Judith, eagerly inquired if she actually intended to give the book to the person who would soonest learn to read it?" His mother repeated the promise, with a smile of joy at the question; the young prince took the book, found out an instructor, and learned to read. When his modesty had crowned his wishes with success, he recited its contents to her. At a subsequent period of his life, he became the great patron of literature; as soon as he had learned Saxon, he studied Latin. He translated many valuable classical and theological works into his native tongue, formed a valuable body of laws, divided the kingdom into shires, established trial by jury, and founded the University of Oxford. His love of poetry remained with him through life, and also his deep gratitude and veneration for the memory of his mother. It is presumed that his delight in minstrelsy arose from his fondness for the songs of the Anglo-Saxon bards. The tones of the harp naturally riveted the attention of the enthusiastic boy. But it was his mother's constant endeavor to impress upon the young prince's mind *the merit of those deeds*, to the recital of which he so early loved to listen, and which he himself, in after life, so gloriously emulated and excelled. Thus Queen Judith not only created in him a love of literature, but what was far better, inspired him with a delight in virtue.

## MOTHER OF JOHN ŒCOLAMPADIUS.

A DISTINGUISHED writer, speaking of the influence of the maternal character, in forming the mind of the child, has said: "There is this remarkable in the strong affections of the mother, in the formation of the literary character, that without ever partaking of, or sympathizing with, the pleasures the child is fond of, the mother will often cherish those first decided tastes, merely from the delight of promoting the happiness of her son: so that genius which some would produce in a preconceived system, or implant by stratagem, or enforce by application, with her may be only the watchful labor of love." This remark was exemplified in reference to the training of John Œcolampadius, the celebrated German reformer. He was born at Winsperg, in Franconia, in the year 1482. His parents were of good family, and in very competent circumstances. His father being a merchant, designed him for his own profession; but his mother was desirous of making him a scholar, and prevailed on her husband to send him to the college of Heilbrun. He was soon removed to the University of Heidelberg, where he received the degree of Bachelor, at fourteen years of age. Thus justifying his mother's presentiment of his talents.

He lived in remarkable and stirring times, and very early made choice of learning as his favorite pursuit and occupation—acquiring languages, and devoting himself to the seclusion of a monastic life, in the monastery of St. Bridget, in the city of Augsburg. It pleased God to call him out of this unwise seclusion, to a more active and useful mode of life. In 1521 he began to go over to the reformers. In 1522 he left his monastery, and went to Basil, in Switzerland, where he was made curate and preacher of the church of St. Martin, and he soon introduced the doctrines of Luther. He was again advanced by the senate to the pastoral office, and now he boldly discovered to his auditors those errors which by continuance had got firm footing in the church. He opened to them the perfection and sufficiency of the merits of Christ. He declared to them the true value of faith, and explained to them the true doctrine of charity, inasmuch, that they began to waver in their minds about the authority of the popish religion. Luther, at this time, was introducing the reformation in Germany, while Zuinglius began to introduce it in Switzerland, by publicly preaching against the corruptions of the Romish Church. Œcolampadius assisted Zuinglius. Upon this foundation he continued preaching, not only against indulgences, but also against the intercession and invocation of saints; the sacrifice of the mass; the ecclesiastical vows; the celibacy of the priests, and the abstinence from meats. However, he did not immediately attempt any alteration in the outward form of public worship, until he found the magistrates and citizens of Zurich disposed to cast off the Romish doctrine, and receive the reformed.

In promoting the vast work of the Protestant Reformation, this distinguished man passed the prime of his days, aiding the cause he had at heart, by his eloquence in the pulpit, and by his pen.   After varied exertions at home and abroad, he returned to Basil, where he spent the remainder of his life in preaching, reading, writing, publishing, visiting the sick, and also the care of certain adjacent churches, till 1531, when it pleased God to visit him with sickness, that soon confined him to his bed, with the greatest appearance of a speedy dissolution.   He surrendered his spirit to his Creator most willingly and cheerfully, on the 1st of December, 1531, and in the forty-ninth year of his age, and was buried, with every mark of respect and concern, in the same city.   He was of a meek and quiet disposition, in the undertaking any business very circumspect, nor was there anything more pleasing to him, than to spend his time in study and contemplation.

---

## THE MOTHER OF FRANCIS LORD BACON.

The writings of Lord Bacon form an era in the literature of our country.   Before the time of this distinguished philosopher, learned men were in the habit of believing all the statements made by the great men of antiquity, respecting the wonders of nature, and the powers of art.   No one thought of examining and inquiring whether these statements were correct;—it was thought enough, if a scholar knew the different systems and opinions of those great men who lived in Greece and Rome, hundreds of years before.   It is obvious no improvement could be made in science, by merely retailing the opinions of others. Lord Bacon was the first to explode this erroneous system, and he taught that all improvement must depend on investigation and experiment—that no man should receive an opinion without testing it. And he advanced this doctrine in a manner so admirable and forcible, that it changed the whole system of study ; and from the time of Lord Bacon until the present, society has been rapidly improving in all the physical sciences, through an adherence to his plan of experiment and personal observation.

The mother of this distinguished man was one of the most learned women that England ever produced. She was the second daughter of Sir Anthony Cook; one of four sisters, all of whom were remarkable for their intellectual attainments ; and the wife of Sir Nicholas Bacon, Lord Keeper of the Great Seal. Lady Bacon was in her youth the governess of Edward the Sixth. He was the first British monarch who was bred up in the reformed faith, and his foundation and endowment of Christ's Hospital, with the scholastic advantages entailed by his liberal views on countless numbers of his youthful countrymen, his astonishing learning, Christian attainments and early death, render his name illustrious in the annals of England.

Lady Bacon had two sons, Nicholas the elder, who became a very eminent man ; and Francis, the future philosopher. Both of them owed the early part of their education to their accomplished mother, and it is admitted, that to her zeal and anxious care—to the pains which she bestowed upon her sons from their earliest infancy, that Francis was mainly indebted for the great reputation that will ever dignify his name. Lord Bacon's veneration for his mother, and his due sense of her valued tuition, was shown by his desire to be interred in the same grave with her, at St. Michael's, near St. Alban's. A striking instance, and a most beautiful example of the advantage that may be derived from maternal influence, early and discreetly exerted over the tender mind of infancy.

---

## WINIFRIDE, MOTHER OF BISHOP HALL.

### BY BISHOP HALL.

My mother, Winifride, of the house of the Bambridges, was a woman of that rare sanctity, that were it not for my interest in nature, I durst say, that neither Aleth, the mother of that just Honor of Clareval, nor Monica, nor any other of those pious matrons, anciently famous for devotion, need to disdain her admittance to comparison. She was continually exercised with the afflictions of a weak body, and oft of a wounded spirit; the agonies whereof, as she would oft recount with much passion, professing that the greatest bodily sickness were but flea-bites to those scorpions; so, from them all, at last she found a happy and comfortable deliverance. And that not without a more than ordinary hand of God: for, on a time, being in great distress of conscience, she thought, in her dream, there stood by her a grave personage, in the gown and other habits of a physician; who inquiring of her estate, and receiving a sad and querulous answer from her, took her by the hand, and bade her be of good comfort, for this should be the last fit that ever she should feel of this kind; whereto she seemed to answer, that, on that condition she could well be content for the time, with that or any other torment; reply was made to her, as she thought, with a redoubled assurance of that happy issue of this her last trial; whereat she began to conceive an unspeakable joy; which yet, on her awaking, left her more disconsolate, as then conceiting her happiness imaginary, her misery real; when, the very same day, she was visited by the reverend and (in his time) famous divine, Mr. Anthony Gilby, under whose ministry she lived: who upon the relation of this her pleasing vision, and the contrary effects it had in her, began to persuade her, that the dream was no other than divine, and that she had good reason to think, that gracious premonition was sent her from God himself: who, though ordinarily he keeps the common road of his proceedings, yet, sometimes, in the distresses of his servants, he goes unusual ways to their relief. Hereupon she began to take heart, and by good counsel and her fervent prayers, found that happy prediction verified to her; and upon all occasions in the remainder of her life, was ready to magnify the mercy of her God in so sensible a deliverance. What with the trial of both these hands of God, so had she profited

in the school of Christ, that it was hard for any friend
to come from her discourse no whit holier. How often
have I blessed the memory of those divine passages of
experimental divinity which I have heard from her
mouth! What day did she pass without a large task
of private devotion? Whence she would still come
forth, with a countenance of undissembled mortification.
Never any lips have read to me such feeling lectures of
piety : neither have I known any soul that more accu-
rately practiced them, than her own. Temptations, de-
sertions, and spiritual comforts, were her usual theme.
Shortly, for I can hardly take off my pen from so exemplary a subject, her life and death were saint-like.

## MRS. ELIZABETH BURNET.

### THE HONORED STEP-MOTHER.

THIS lady was born November 8th, in the year 1661.
She was the eldest daughter of Sir Richard Blake,
Knight, the fifth son of Thomas Blake, Esq., of Earon-
toun, in the county of Southampton, of an eminent
family, and of Elizabeth, daughter of Dr. Bathurst, a
physician in London, a person of distinguished piety,
and among the most considerable men of his profession
in his time.

At eleven years old, she began to have a true sense
of religion, and read with great application the books
that were put into her hands; but was not entirely
satisfied with them, aspiring after more solid and sub-

3*

lime sentiments than what she met with in them.   On this account it was, that more than ordinary care was taken to make her think meanly of herself, she being bred up in the greatest privacy possible.

When she was but little more than seventeen years of age, she was married to Robert Berkely, Esq., of Spetchly, in the county of Worcester, grandson of Sir Robert Berkely, who was a Judge in the reign of Charles II.  The match between this young gentleman and her was procured principally by means of Dr. Fell, then Bishop of Oxford, was Mr. Berkely's guardian, and had taken the care of his education.  The Bishop thought that the assisting his friend in that match was the greatest service he ever performed for him.  He contracted an intimate friendship with the eminent Dr. Stillingfleet, bishop of Worcester, who, to his death, maintained a high regard for her; and upon several occasions, has been often heard to say, " that he knew not a more considerable woman in England than she was."  Thus she continued to live with Mr. Berkely, till the year 1693, when it pleased God to remove him from her by death.

In her widowhood, as she had more leisure than in her married state, so she applied it wholly to devotion, to reading, to acts of charity, and the offices of friendship.  Particularly, she took upon her the care of her late husband's Protestant relations, as if they had been her own; and, indeed, she was a mother to them all as long as she lived, and showed a great concern and kindness for them at her death.  She was also very good and obliging to all the rest of his family. She had then a very plentiful income, which she managed with great prudence, as well as in a large exercise of charity : and, indeed, she was uneasy at all other kind of expenses but what went in that way. While she continued at Spetchly, she kept a hospitable table, to which the neighboring clergy were always welcome. She paid true respect to such of them as were in low circumstances, cordially esteeming them for their functions and labors. She frequently made them presents of the most useful books, and to some she generously lent money, without requiring any security, expecting only to be paid when, by the providence of God, they might be put into more easy circumstances.

She continued a widow nearly seven years, and then was married to Dr. Gilbert Burnet, Bishop of Salisbury. She found in the Bishop's house a family of children, whom she treated, not with a false indulgence on the one hand, nor with unnatural severity on the other hand; but with all that care and true concern for their education, as if they had been her own; and, indeed, she was loved and respected by them as if she had brought them into the world : of which the Bishop was so sensible, that he had, by his will then made, left them under her direction and authority in so absolute a manner, that it has been seldom known that so much power was ever entrusted even to the real mothers of any children.

The Bishop, rightly judging that he brought blessing and happiness enough into his family by bringing such a mother into it, desired her to secure all her own estate and income to herself, with a power to make such a will as she pleased, to which he bound himself to consent.

Thus she continued the mistress of all that was her own, allowing for her own entertainment what did not exceed the rate of a boarding-house, that she might the more abound in good works; which the Bishop accepted of, though he was willing, as he often told her, "that nothing at all should be allowed on that account." After this, she extended her charity further than she had done before; and instead of giving a fifth part of her income, which would have been no small proportion, she was very uneasy at taking only a fifth part to her own use. She seldom went beyond it, and was much oftener restrained within it, by which means she was enabled to employ considerable sums in charitable uses; particularly the number of children taught at her expense, in and about Worcester and Salisbury, amounting to above a hundred.

To be rich in good works, was visibly the reigning design of her whole life, and that in which she most of all delighted herself.

This excellent woman kept a constant journal of her life, and every evening employed no inconsiderable time in recollecting her actions and discourse in the day; and she would call herself to an account in every particular, that the errors of days past might be avoided in those that might follow. She died February 3, 1709.

REV. OLIVER HEYWOOD, A.M., AND HIS MOTHER.

THIS eminent Nonconformist divine was born March, 1829, in Little Lever, in the Parish of Bolton. His parents were pious and respectable; and accordingly, he, along with his eight brothers and three sisters, were trained up in the fear of the Lord. But, however judiciously conducted, early education is not always sufficient to restrain the united propensities of the human heart; and in the case of Oliver Heywood, the truth of this remark was strikingly exemplified. He himself bears testimony to the waywardness and improper conduct of his youthful days:—"Then," says he, "one of my sisters found fault with me for profane swearing: I replied, 'I had not sworn so much as a neighbor's child, with whom I used to play;' so foolish was I, and ignorant. How fond was I of trifles! How awkward to good exercises! How forward to sinful practices! How easily led to follow bad examples! I may say, 'childhood and youth are vanity; yea, next akin to brutish stupidity, and atheistical blasphemy.' 'When I was a child, I spake as a child;' yea, rather like a devil incarnate. O! the desperate wickedness of my deceitful heart!"

At length, it pleased God to awaken his mind to a sense of the importance of religion, and to call him effectually "out of darkness into God's marvelous light." The instructions of his affectionate parents were not lost upon him, but, by the Divine blessing, they proved the means of preserving him from the destruction into which he was but too obviously rushing. In his mother, he seems to have been more especially indebted for the knowledge of divine things, which he acquired in youth, and this he readily owned in after life. "I may say," to quote his words, "I owe much to her, as the instrument, under God, of that saving good I at first received, and I hope I shall never forget the instructions of a mother." He early showed an inclination to prepare for the important and highly responsible office of a minister of the Gospel. In his eighteenth year, accordingly, he was sent to Cambridge, where, besides prosecuting his studies with diligence and success, he enjoyed the opportunity of attending the faithful ministry of the celebrated Dr. Hammond. The ministrations of this distinguished divine were much blessed to him, as well as to many other students at the same time. Several of these pious young men were in the habit of meeting together frequently, for prayer and mutual edification.

Mr. Heywood was desirous to obtain a scholarship, with the view of contributing toward his own support at college; and in all probability he would have obtained it, had he not been arrested in his studies by a severe fever, which reduced him so low, that he was not expected to live.

In his sickness he solemnly vowed to the Lord, that if his life should be spared, he would dedicate it to the service of the sanctuary. A vow which he accordingly performed, with the earnest desire of winning souls to the Redeemer.

## MRS. CATHERINE CLARKE'S MOTHER.

### WIFE OF THE REV. SAMUEL CLARKE.

CATHERINE OVERTON was born at Bedworth, in the county of Warwick, four miles from Coventry, February 25th, 1602, of religious parents. Her father was Mr. Valentine Overton, rector of Bedworth, where he lived a constant and diligent preacher of God's holy word, till he was almost eighty-two years of age. Her mother's maiden name was Isaverton: she was a most excellent woman, who took the whole burden of family affairs, both within and without doors, from off her husband, that he might with the more freedom attend his holy calling.

On February 2nd, 1625, (the same day on which King Charles I. was crowned,) she was, with the consent of parents on both sides, married to Mr. S. Clarke, at that time minister of Shotwick, four miles beyond West Chester, who looked upon this match as the greatest outward temporal blessing that ever God bestowed upon him; whereby he could experimentally say, "that a prudent wife is the gift of God," and that in the possession of her he enjoyed more mercies than he could well enumerate.

Her piety was signal and exemplary. She was a constant and diligent attendant on the public ministry of God's holy word; and when she lived where she had the opportunity of hearing lectures in the week day, she made choice to attend upon those who were most plain, practical, and powerful preachers; and when days of humiliation and thanksgiving came, she never failed to make one among God's people in the celebration of them. The Lord's days she carefully sanctified, both in public and in private, rising earlier upon them than upon others, especially when she had many young children about her, that so she might have opportunity as well for secret as for family duties, before she was called away to the public. She was, like David's doorkeeper, one of the first in and last out of God's house. Her constant posture at prayer was kneeling, thinking that she could not be too humble before God. Her usual manner was to write sermons, to prevent drowsiness and distractions, and to help memory. Of these she has left many volumes; and her practice was to make good use of them, by frequent reading and meditating upon them: and if at any time she was cast into such places and company as were a hinderance to her, in the strict sanctification of this holy day, it was a grief and burden to her.

As a mother to her children, whereof God gave her nine—four sons and five daughters—she was most exemplary, nursing them all herself. She loved them dearly without fondness; was careful to give them nurture as well as nourishment, not sparing the rod when there was just occasion, and as soon as they were capable, she was vigilant and diligent to season their tender years with grace and virtue, *by instilling into their minds the first grounds and principles of religion ;* and as they grew up, she did more freely discover her tender affection for them, by instruction, advice, and good counsel, as there was occasion; and when they were disposed of abroad, she labored, by her gracious letters and hearty instructions at their meetings, to build them up in grace and godliness;—and God was pleased to let her see, to her great joy and comfort, the fruit of her prayers and pains, in keeping them from scandalous courses, and in working grace in most of their hearts.

Her youngest son taking his leave of her the day before her death, she gave him much heavenly counsel for the good of his soul, and blessed him, and all his, as she did the rest of her children and grand-children. She earnestly desired to be dissolved, and breathed after a fuller enjoyment of Jesus Christ, which she accounted best of all. She would sometimes say, "that it was a hard thing to die; and this is a hard work."

Her understanding, memory, and speech continued till within two minutes of death; and a little before, her daughter speaking to her of Jesus Christ, she replied, "My God and my Lord;" and so, June 21st, 1675, about five o'clock in the morning, she fell asleep, exchanging this life for a better, without any alteration in her countenance, but only that her color was gone. She closed up her eyes herself, as she would say, "It is but winking, and I shall be in heaven." She "changed her place, but not her company." She was seventy-three years and about four months of age, and had been married about fifty years.

4

## SIR ISAAC NEWTON'S MOTHER.

SIR ISAAC NEWTON, the great, the learned, and the good; who followed in the track of his illustrious predecessor, Sir Francis Bacon, styled by Walpole, "the prophet of arts which Newton was afterward to reveal," was indebted to maternal solicitude for the development of that genius which has never since been surpassed, nor ever equaled.

Unlike Lord Bacon, however, the immortal Newton had no illustrious father to pave the way for his son's celebrity: he had no learned and accomplished mother to direct his infant mind to principles of science, at the time when it was most susceptible of imbibing them. He knew not the blessing even of a father's encouragement, for it was the fate of this great philosopher to be a posthumous child, and so sickly and diminutive was he at birth, that little hope was entertained of preserving his life.

But Newton, though not blessed with learned parents, possessed a devout and Christian mother, whose sole aim and study was to sow the seeds of piety and virtue in his mind, and whose tender care preserved to us, under God's blessing, one destined to be the glory of his country, and his race.

Sir Isaac Newton was born in 1642, and about the time he attained his fourth year his mother married, secondly, a clergyman; but she did not suffer this alliance to interfere with her duties to her son.

When the watchful attention of maternal love had strengthened his feeble constitution, and her judicious instruction had invigorated the dawning powers of his intellect, she sent him to school to be taught the classics ; but having given him such few scholastic advantages as she considered sufficient for the inheritor of a small patrimony, she again withdrew him to his home to be initiated into the management of a farm, that, like his ancestors, he might be devoted to a country life. But, for the retirement thus afforded—a retirement so suited to foster the reflective powers of his expanding mind—Newton perhaps had never been led to those contemplative habits which afterward produced his immortal theory of universal gravitation ; for though, at the instance of his uncle, he had been previously removed to Cambridge for mathematical instruction, yet the predisposition of the young philosopher for metaphysics was encouraged, if not originally induced, by that previous retirement, which was almost forced upon him by the prudence and affection of his anxious mother.

Great, indeed, are the obligations of literature to the mother whose untiring watchfulness in infancy preserved the life of so great a man, and whose gentle sway allowed him in childhood perfect freedom of thought and action, save in the one point peculiarly apportioned to a mother's care, the task of inculcating the truths of our holy religion—a task never more beautifully illustrated than by its result ; for Sir Isaac Newton was not only a philosopher, but a Christian,

and spent much of his time in elucidating the sacred
Scriptures; nor could anything discompose his mind
so much as light and irreverent expressions on the subject of religion.   The illustrious son and the pious
mother were equally worthy of each other.

---

REV. THOMAS HALYBURTON AND HIS MOTHER.

This distinguished man, who became professor of divinity in the University of St. Andrew's, was born at
Duplin, near Perth, December the 25th, 1674.   His
father, formerly minister of that parish, was ejected,
with about three hundred others, for nonconformity.
Both his parents were eminently pious.   In 1682, his
father died, in the fifty-ninth year of his age; and the
care of his son's morals and education devolved on his
*excellent mother*.

Never was the union of piety and literature in the
maternal character more fully developed than in this
instance.   But for this, the world might never have
heard, nor the church have felt the benefit of the talents and Christian virtues of a Halyburton.   This
excellent woman was the mother of eleven children,
out of which number she followed nine to the grave at
a very early age.   In addition to her other trials, she
was driven, by the rage of persecution, to seek an
asylum in Holland for herself and her children, two of
which only were now left to her—the subject of the
present sketch, and her eldest daughter, who was
married.

While on his voyage to Holland, he speaks in his memoirs of various convictions arising in his mind in times of real or apprehended danger, but acknowledges at the same time that he knew nothing of acceptance and communion with God, and attributes his concern of mind to a mixture of natural fear and a selfish desire of preservation from supposed danger. He made resolutions in the storm which subsided with the winds, and corruption that had been dammed in for a little, having forced down the temporary mounds that had been raised against it, broke its way with increased violence and force. Having reached land and fixed at Rotterdam, he was, by the care of his ever watchful mother, placed within reach of the most valuable instructions of one of the suffering ministers.

In the month of February, 1687, King James issued his proclamations for indulgences, when most of those who had fled returned home, and his mother and family amongst them. During the voyage, they were in imminent danger of shipwreck, but providentially escaped. This danger being sudden, left but little impression on Halyburton's mind. He took up his abode with his mother at Perth, till 1690 or 1691. Being placed under good scholastic discipline, he made considerable proficiency. But religion, as yet, made no effective impression on his mind, till toward the close of James' reign, when the fear of a massacre, or some sudden stroke from the papists, revived his concern for his eternal welfare. This was aided by evangelical instructions from his mother, increased knowledge and

4*

seasons of sickness, and more especially by the state of public affairs. His fear of the dangers of the papists having ceased through the battle of Killiecrankie, his remaining difficulty was only with his convictions, which he could by no means effect for any considerable length of time together. He began to be perplexed respecting the evidences of revealed religion, till after having experienced some mental relief from Robert Bruce's "Fulfilling the Scriptures:" he received further relief from Mr. Donaldson, an excellent old minister, who came to preach at Perth, and paid a visit to his mother. He inquired of his young friend, if he sought a blessing from God on his learning, remarking at the same time, with an austere look, "Sirrah, unsanctified learning has done much mischief to the Kirk of God." This led him to seek Divine direction in extraordinary difficulties; but this exercise, he acknowledges, left him still afar off from God. In 1690 or 91, his mother removed to Edinburgh, and placed him at Mr. Gavin Weir's school, where he remained (a short interval excepted) till November, 1692, when he entered the college, under Mr. Alexander Cunningham. Here his convictions increased, chiefly through the means of sermons from the pulpit, and the private perusal of Shepherd's "Sincere Convert." His formal attention to the duties of the closet increased, but no solid peace was yet attained, till, about this time, meeting with Clarke's "Martyrology," and being naturally fond of history, he read it with eager attention, and received many valuable impressions which never left him. In

May, 1693, he was advised, on his mother's account, as well as his own, to seek a change of air, and they went to St. Andrew's, where he entered college. He was placed under the care of Mr. Thomas Taylor, a man of learning, and who was exceedingly kind to him. At St. Andrew's, his regard for religion increased; and under the ministry of Mr. Thomas Forrester, he began to discover the secret evils of his heart. He formed many good resolutions, and thought he had found peace; but it was a structure which had for its foundation vows, made and sometimes fulfilled, with apparent success, rather than the atonement of Christ. Having applied himself closely, three years, to the study of philosophy, he had thought of going abroad in search of further improvement; but fear of the sea on the one hand, and the pressing solicitation of friends on the other, prevailed with him to engage as domestic chaplain in a nobleman's family. Accordingly, in August, 1696, he went to the Wemyes. Here he met with considerable difficulties, arising out of his prominent situation, and more especially from the debates into which he was drawn on the truth of religion.

In resorting to the works of Deists, with a view to meet their arguments, his own mind was much perplexed, but the valuable fruit of his study, in reference to others, may be seen in his admirable "Treatise on Deism." Nor, in the end, could he regret a research which taught him an humble submission to the dictates of Divine revelation, notwithstanding, at present, he was the subject of the most distressing doubts. He represents his state of depression, during this conflict, as of a nature too grave to have been long sustained. But early in the year 1698, he obtained from the Scriptures that salutary relief, which was no less necessary to his earthly existence, than to his spiritual peace. New light broke in upon his mind. From the doctrine of the cross he derived that consolation which he had in vain sought elsewhere, and that purity which is connected, as a principle, with the religion of Christ. His heart was expanded toward others, and for many days together, he says, "he seemed admitted into the very 'secret of the Divine pavilion.'" The most overwhelming sense of his own worthlessness pervaded his mind, and his feelings of reverence for God were unusually exalted. "His joy he states to have been 'truly unspeakable, and full of glory.'" So much was he raised above earth, that he could scarcely bend his mind to the perusal of any works but those of a devotional character. His views of the enormity of sin, he says, "grew clearer as he advanced in holiness : his contrition under it became more pungent, and his desire after freedom from its influence more ardent." All his former doubts respecting the being of a God vanished in the clear light of an evangelical faith ; and he had a witness to the existence of a Being, of infinite love and purity, in the internal satisfaction and holiness of his heart. The bulky arguments that appeared as mountains, "shook at the presence of the Lord, and were carried into the midst of the sea."

The authenticity of the Scriptures, which he had pre-

viously disputed, and which could be removed neither
by personal investigation, nor by reading the works of
others, now received sufficient proof in the discoveries
which they had enabled him to make of his own guilt,
of the being, attributes, and purposes of God; and the
transforming, quickening, supporting, and reviving influences which they communicated to his own mind.
In short, reason now became entirely the disciple of
revelation, and the thoughts of entering the ministry,
which he had previously laid aside, on account of the
wavering state of his mind, now returned. In April
or May, 1698, two ministers from the presbytery of
Kirkaldy visited him, and pressed him to enter on trial
for the ministry. He objected his want of reading, of
a knowledge of language, etc.; but after repeated solicitations, he complied, and was licensed by them to
preach, June the 22d, 1699. He was appointed minister of Ceres parish, May 1st, 1700. Within a few
years after his settlement at Ceres, his health began to
fail; and at length his indisposition so much increased,
that with great difficulty he went through the labors
incident to so large a parish. In April, 1710, he was
appointed, by patent from Queen Anne, professor of
divinity in the new college of St. Andrew's, through
the mediation of the Synod of Fife, and delivered his
inaugural address, in confutation of an atheistical pam-
phlet.

In April, 1711, he was seized with a dangerous
pleurisy. This disease was removed, but he never
fully recovered his former strength; and on the 23d

of September, 1712, he departed triumphantly to his
eternal rest. His last words are among the richest
features which piety ever bequeathed to the church;
and the letters which he dedicated on his dying bed
are specimens of his devotion and concern for the welfare of others. He was singularly fitted for the schools.
He spoke elegant Latin with fluency: he was well
skilled in Greek, but his sickness prevented the execution of his design to learn the oriental languages. Few
lives have been more useful and distinguished by genuine piety: his death was a loss to Scotland, and the
world at large. His works, in addition to those already mentioned, consist of, "The Great Concern of
Salvation," in three parts.

Ten sermons preached before and after the celebration of the Lord's Supper; to which are added, two
sermons, preached upon occasion of the death of a
friend. To these discourses is prefixed an excellent
preface by Dr. Watts, highly expressive both of their
own worth, and of their author's.

---

### DR. SAMUEL JOHNSON AND HIS MOTHER.

OF the power of his memory, for which he was all his
life eminent to a degree almost incredible, the following early instance was told me in his presence, at
Litchfield, in 1776, by his step-daughter, Mrs. Lucy
Potter, as related to her, by his mother.

When he was a child in petticoats, and had learnt

to read, Mrs. Johnson one morning put the Common Prayer Book into his hands, pointed to the collect for the day, and said, "Sam, you must get this by heart." She went up stairs, leaving him to study it; but by the time she had reached the second floor, she heard him following her. "What's the matter?" said she; "I can say it," he replied, and repeated it distinctly, though he could not have read it more than twice.

It is related of the mother of this distinguished man, that when he was a young child, of three or four years old, that his mother used often to tell him some religious truth or moral mixim, and she required of him that he should go and tell the servant-maid what he had heard;—by this simple but admirable plan his memory was strengthened and exercised, and a yet more valuable faculty was called into use, namely, a facility of communicating, in language of his own, the truths he had just been taught.

Dr. Johnson, when advanced in life, speaking of his boyhood, said, "When I was a youth, and used to argue with my mother on various points, I used to take the wrong side of an argument, because it was that on which the most ingenious things could be said." Perhaps none but a mother, and that a kind one, could have borne with the waywardness and perversity of a boy acting on such a plan; instead, however, of cutting him short with a reproof, she entered into his humor, argued the matter out with him, and thus gave him an opportunity of exercising his ingenuity as a disputant.

Dr. Johnson, in after life, was celebrated for his conversational powers. Is it not probable this early training was the means of aiding in the development of his colloquial fluency ?

In 1759, in the month of January, his mother died at the great age of ninety, an event which deeply affected him ; not that his mind had acquired no firmness by the contemplation of mortality, but that his reverential affection for her was not abated by years, as, indeed, he retained all his tender feelings even to the latest period of his life.

A friend was told that he regretted much his not having gone to visit his mother for several years previous to her death. But he was constantly engaged in literary labors, which confined him to London ; and though he had not the comfort of seeing his aged parent, he contributed liberally to her support.

Soon after this event, he wrote his " Rasselas, Prince of Abyssinia ;" concerning the publication of which Sir John Hawkins guesses vaguely and idly, instead of having taken the trouble to inform himself with authentic precision. Not to trouble my readers with a repetition of the Knight's reveries, I have to mention, that the late Mr. Strahan, the printer, stated that Johnson wrote it, that with the profits he might defray the expense of his mother's funeral, and pay some little debts which she had left. He told Sir Joshua Reynolds, that he composed it in the evenings of one week—sent it to the press in portions as it was written, and had never since read it over. Mr. Strahan, Mr.

Johnson, and Mr. Dodsley, purchased it for a hundred pounds, but afterward paid him twenty-five pounds more when it came to a second edition.

---

## PRESIDENT EDWARDS AND HIS MOTHER.

JONATHAN EDWARDS was born at East Windsor, on the banks of the Connecticut, on the 5th day of October, 1703. His father was the Rev. Timothy Edwards, a most diligent and exemplary pastor, and a distinguished scholar. *His mother was a woman of very extensive information, of a thorough knowledge of the Scriptures, and of fervent piety.* The education of Jonathan was of a very superior character. Brought up "in the nurture and admonition of the Lord;" under the care of parents at once strict and affectionate, he was preserved, in a great degree, from the company of bad companions, and from those "evil communications" which too often prove the ruin of the young. Even in early life, however, he seems to have been characterized by firmness and sedateness, and a sound and discriminating judgment. Blessed with enlightened parents, they taught him from childhood to exercise and strengthen his intellectual faculties, by cultivating an acquaintance with all the objects of contemplation within his reach. Their faithful religious instructions, too, rendered him, while yet a child, conversant with his own character and duties, with the way of salvation by Jesus Christ, and the nature of that eternal

5

life which, begun on earth, is perfected in heaven.
Like faithful servants of their divine Master, they not
only pointed out the road that conducts to the mansions
of bliss, but they showed him examples of perseverance
therein, and sought for him, by constant prayer, the
guidance of that Great Being, who alone can lead " in
the way everlasting."

Their prayers for their son commenced with his very
existence, and like every prayer of faith, they were
answered and secured for him at an early period of
life—the peculiar blessing of God. While yet very
young, Edwards experienced powerful religious impressions, and especially before he went to college, during
an extensive revival of religion in his father's congregation. These impressions, however, ultimately disap-
peared, and, in his own opinion, were followed by no
permanent effects of a salutary nature.

In his early years, he seems to have been fond of
the use of the pen, and the vigor, and the shrewdness,
and the sound judgment displayed in some pieces
which he composed before he had attained his twelfth
year, are almost incredible. They display, in an astonishing degree, those very qualities which so distinguished him in after life ; and show how much truth
there is in the poet's remark :—

" The child is father of the man."

Any eulogy on the immortal Edwards is unnecessary.

### MRS. WESLEY AND HER CHILDREN.[1]

MRS. WESLEY was assiduous in teaching her children their duty to God and to their parents. She had nineteen children, most of whom lived to be educated. *All these were educated by herself!* Their times of going to bed, rising in the morning, dressing, eating, learning, and exercise, she managed by rule, which was never suffered to be broken. From her, Mr. John Wesley derived all that knowledge in the education of children which he has detailed so simply, and so successfully enforced. It has been considered that a man who had no children of his own, could not have known so well how they should be managed and educated; but that wonder will at once cease when it is recollected who was his instructress in all things during his infancy and youth.

Mrs. Wesley had little difficulty in breaking the wills of her children. They were early brought, by rational means, under a mild yoke; they were perfectly obsequious to their parents, and were taught to wait their decision in everything they were to have, and in everything they were to perform. They were taught, also, to ask a blessing upon their food, to behave quietly at family prayers, and to reverence the Sabbath. They were never permitted to command the servants, to use any words of authority, in their addresses to them.

Mrs. Wesley charged the servants to do nothing for

[1] From Dr. Adam Clarke's Memoir of the Wesley Family.

any of the children, unless they asked it with humility and respect; and the children were duly informed that the servants had such orders. "Molly,—Robert, be pleased to do so and so," was the usual method of request, both from the sons and daughters; and because the children behaved thus decently, the domestics reverenced and loved them; were strictly attentive to, and felt it a privilege to serve them.

They were never permitted to contend with each other: whatever difficulties arose, the parents decided, and their decision was never disputed. The consequence was, there were few misunderstandings among them, and no unbrotherly or vindictive passions; and they had the common fame of being the most loving family in the county of Lincoln.

How much evil may be prevented, and how much good may be done, by judicious management in the education of children!

Mrs. Wesley has explained her own views and conduct in a letter, dated July 24th, 1732, part of which is here given. "In order to form the minds of children, the first thing to be done is to conquer their will, and bring them to an obedient temper. To inform the understanding is a work of time, and must, with children, proceed by slow degrees, as they are able to bear it; but the subjecting the will is a thing that must be done at once, and the sooner the better; for by neglecting timely correction, they will correct a stubbornness and obstinacy which are hardly ever after conquered, and never without using such severity as would

be as painful to me as to the child.   In the esteem of
the world, they pass for kind and indulgent, whom I
call cruel parents; who permit their children to get
habits which they know must be afterward broken.
Nay, some are so stupidly fond, as in sport to teach
their children to do things which, in a while afterward,
they have severely beaten them for doing.   When a
child is corrected, it must be conquered, and this will
be no hard matter to do, if it be not grown headstrong
by too much indulgence.   And when the will of a child
is totally subdued, and it is brought to revere and stand
in awe of its parents, then a great many childish follies
and inadvertencies must be passed by—some should be
overlooked, and taken no notice of; and others mildly
reproved; but no sinful transgression ought ever to be
forgiven children, without chastisement less or more,
as the nature and circumstances of the offence may
require.   I insist upon conquering the will of children
betimes, because this is the only strong and rational
foundation of a religious education, without which, both
precept and example will be ineffectual.   But when
this is thoroughly done, then a child is capable of being
governed by the reason and piety of its parents, till its
own understanding comes to maturity, and the principles of religion have taken root in the mind.   I cannot
yet dismiss this subject.   As self-will is the root of all
sin and misery, so, whatever cherishes this in children,
insures their after wretchedness and irreligion; whatever checks and mortifies it, promotes their future happiness and piety.

5*

This is still more evident, if we further consider that religion is nothing else than the doing the will of God, and not our own; that the one grand impediment to our temporal and eternal happiness, being thus self-will, no indulgence of it can be trivial, no denial unprofitable : so that the parent who studies to subdue it in his child, works together with God, in the renewing and saving a soul. The parent who indulges it, does the devil's work; makes religion impracticable; salvation unattainable ; and does all that in him lies to damn his child, body and soul, forever."

So wise, judicious, and affectionate a mother, was worthy of those illustrious sainted sons, the influence of whose learning and piety will bless mankind to the latest posterity.

---

### MRS. SAVAGE AND HER CHILDREN.[1]

SHE loved home, and as the head of a family, aimed, by setting a pattern of cheerful, serious piety, to walk "as becometh the Gospel." For the spiritual welfare of her domestics she cherished a holy zeal, and discovered it by regular and patient instruction, as well as fervent prayer. "Oh!" she writes soon after her marriage, "that the family might be the better for me. As far as I know my own heart, I earnestly desire the salvation of every soul under our roof. Oh,

[1] From Williams's Life of Mrs. Savage.

that they did but see what I see of the excellency of
Christ, the sinfulness of sin, and the vanity of creatures."

She was the mother of nine children. The care and
tenderness she discovered in their infancy, did not exceed her concern for their souls. As they advanced
in years, her pious anxiety increased, and no pains were
spared to teach them the things of God. A considerable portion of the evening of the Sabbath was devoted
to family instruction. She excelled in the happy art
of recommending religion to the young. She gained
their attention, and encouraged them to be inquisitive
in divine subjects. To her instructions were added the
most affectionate prayers; and her children, who were
not immediately under her inspection, were visited with
such letters of piety and love as, with the blessing of
God, were calculated to produce the happiest effects.
Her diary abounds with expressions of concern for her
children. "Oh!" she writes, "that I could be every
day travailing to see Christ formed in them. This
week I was much affected when, reading in course,
Proverbs xxx. 8, 'Remove far from me vanity and
lies.' Methinks it is a very proper prayer for children.
I have earnestly begged of God to remove from mine
'vanity and lies.'" At another time, "I read in
course in my closet, Isaiah liv., with the exposition; I
was much affected with the 13th verse, 'And all thy children shall be taught of the Lord.' Though it is spoken
of the Church's children, I could apply it to my own
children in particular, and desire to act faith on it. I
am caring and endeavoring that they may be taught

and instructed in the good way. This is the inward desire of my soul. 'Now, saith God, they shall be taught of *me*, and *all* thy children shall: a sweet promise; it much satisfies me.' Lord, set in with poor parents, who desire nothing in the world so much as to see their children walk in the 'narrow way that leads to life.'"

---

## COLONEL GARDINER AND HIS MOTHER.

### BY DR. DODDRIDGE.

MRS. GARDINER, the mother of Col. Gardiner, was a lady of a very valuable character. She was, indeed, exercised with uncommon trials; but it pleased God to bless these various and heavy afflictions as the means of forming her to that eminent degree of piety which will render her memory dear and honorable to the good, as long as it remains. James, her second son, of whom some account is now to be given, was born at Carriden, in Linlithgowshire, Jan. 10th, 1687. His mother took care to instruct him, with great tenderness and affection, in the principles of Christianity. The good effects of her prudent and exemplary care were not so conspicuous as she desired and hoped, in the younger part of her son's life; yet there is great reason to believe that it was not in vain. He had many convictions and restraints, even while going on in the ways of wickedness, which probably arose, through grace, from these early instructions; and when religious impressions

took that hold of his heart which they afterward did,
that stock of knowledge which was laid up in his mind
during his childhood, proved of the greatest service.
And I have heard him make the observation, as an encouragement to parents and other pious friends to do
their duty, and to hope for those good consequences
of it which may not immediately appear.

He had also a very religious aunt, of whose good
instructions and exhortations he often spoke with pleasure, after he became sensible of their value.   Neither
of those venerable relatives could dissuade him from a
military life.   Indeed, his spirit was so rash and un-
governable, that he fought three duels before he had
attained to the stature of a man.   After his remarkable conversion, his sentiments on this subject were so
much changed, that he declined a challenge, with this
calm and noble reply:—" I fear sinning, though you
know I do not fear fighting."   However, he went on for
many years in a daring course of disobedience and im-
piety, neither fearing God, nor regarding man.   Though
he was exposed to many dangers as an officer abroad,
and was often delivered in a surprising manner, yet he
manifested no thankfulness to his great Preserver, but
continued to wallow in the mire of iniquity.   Yet still,
the checks of conscience, and some remaining principles
of so good an education, would break in upon his most
licentious hours; and I particularly remember he told
me, that when some of his dissolute companions were
once congratulating him on his distinguished felicity, a
dog happening at that time to come into the room, he

could not forbear groaning inwardly, and saying to himself : " O ! that I were that dog !"  So true is it, that " there is no peace to the wicked."  When men pursue brutal pleasures, they will not even afford them brutal happiness.  Notwithstanding these feelings of disappointment and remorse, he ran to such lengths of sin in this wretched part of his life, that some gentlemen, who made no great pretences to religion, declined his company, lest they should be ensnared and corrupted by it.  During this course of sin and folly, he was never a skeptic in his principles, but still retained a secret apprehension that both natural and revealed religion— though he did not much care to think of either—were founded in truth.  His continual neglect of the Great Author of his being, of whose perfections he could not doubt, and to whom he knew himself to be under daily and perpetual obligations, gave him, in some moments of reflection, inexpressible remorse, which wrought upon him to such a degree, that he resolved he would attempt to pay Him some acknowledgments.  Accordingly, for a few mornings he did it, repeating in retirement some passages out of the Psalms, and perhaps other Scriptures, which he still retained on his memory ; and owning in a few strong words the many mercies and deliverances he had received, and the ill returns he had made for them.  But these strains were too devout to continue long in a heart, as yet, quite unsanctified.  He was stopped short by the remonstrances of his conscience, showing him the flagrant absurdity of confessing sins he did not desire to forsake, and of pretending to praise

God for his mercies when he did not evidence sincere
gratitude in his life.   The use of such language before
a heart-searching God, merely as a hypocritical form,
while the sentiments of his soul were contrary to it,
justly appeared to him such daring profaneness, that
deeply depraved as his mind then was, the very thought
of it struck him with horror.   He therefore determined
to lay aside prayer.   These efforts at devotion would
sometimes return, but they were overborne again and
again by the force of temptation, and his heart grew
still harder.   Nor was it softened or awakened by some
very remarkable deliverances which, at this time, he
received.   Going down a hill on horseback, the animal
threw him off and pitched over him; so that, when he
rose, the horse lay beyond him almost dead.   Yet,
though he did not sustain even the least injury, it made
no serious impression on his mind.   A few weeks
afterward, as he was returning to England in the
packet-boat, a violent storm arose, and tossed them for
several hours, in a dark night, on the coast of Holland.
At length they were brought into such an extremity,
that the captain of the vessel urged him to go to prayers immediately, if he ever intended to go at all; for
he concluded, they would in a few minutes be at the
bottom of the sea.   In this alarming situation he did
pray, and that very fervently, too; and it was remarkable, that while he was crying to God for deliverance,
the wind fell; and quickly after they arrived at Calais.
But the major was so little affected with what had be-
fallen him, that when some of his gay friends, on hear-

ing the story, rallied him upon the efficacy of his prayers, he excused himself from being thought much in
earnest, by saying, "that it was midnight, and an hour
when his good mother and aunt were asleep, or else
he would have left that part of the business to them."
Thus did he pour his contempt upon devotion, and
upon those excellent relatives, to whose prayers and
endeavors he was so greatly indebted. His great deliverance from the powers of darkness was now nearly
approaching. He recounted these things to me with
the greatest humility, as showing how utterly unworthy he was of the miracle of Divine grace, by which
he was, quickly after, brought to so powerful a sense
of religion. This memorable event happened toward
the middle of July, 1719. The major had spent the
evening (and, if I mistake not, it was the Sabbath) in
some gay company, and had formed a criminal engagement to be attended at twelve o'clock. The company
broke up about eleven, when he went into his chamber
to kill the tedious hour by reading some amusing book.
But it happened that he took up a religious book,
which his good mother or aunt had, without his knowledge, slipped into his portmanteau. It was called, if
I remember the title exactly, "The Christian Soldier,
or Heaven taken by Storm;" it was written by Mr. T.
Watson. Guessing, by the title of it, that he should
find phrases of his own profession spiritualized, in a
manner which he thought might afford him some diversion, he resolved to dip into it; but he took no
serious notice of anything he read in it; and yet, while

this book was in his hand, an impression was made upon his mind (perhaps only God knows how) which drew after it a train of the most important and happy consequences.    He thought he saw an unusual blaze of light fall upon the book which he was reading, which he at first imagined might happen by some accident in the candle.    But lifting up his eyes, he apprehended, to his extreme amazement, that there was before him, as it were, suspended in the air a visible representation of the Lord Jesus Christ upon the cross, surrounded on all sides with a glory; and was impressed as if a voice had come to this effect:—" Oh! sinner, did I suffer this for thee, and are these thy returns?"    Struck with so amazing a phenomenon as this, there remained hardly any life in him, so that he sunk down in the arm-chair in which he sat, and continued, he knew not exactly how long, insensible.    At length he rose in a tumult of passions not to be conceived, and walked to and fro in his chamber, till he was ready to drop down in unutterable astonishment and agony; appearing to himself the vilest monster in the creation of God, who had all his life-time been crucifying Christ afresh by his sins, and now assuredly saw, by a miraculous vision, the horror of what he had done.    With this was connected such a view of the majesty and goodness of God, as caused him to abhor himself, and to repent as in dust and ashes.    He immediately gave judgment against himself, that he was most justly worthy of eternal damnation.    He passed the remainder of the night waking, and could get but little rest in several

6

that followed.  His mind was constantly taken up in reflecting on the Divine purity and goodness; the grace which had been proposed to him in the Gospel, and which he had rejected; the singular advantages he had neglected and abused; and the many favors of providence which he had received, particularly in rescuing him from so many imminent dangers of death, which he now saw must have been followed with such dreadful and hopeless destruction.  The privileges of his education, which he had so much despised, now lay with an almost insupportable weight upon his mind; and the folly of that career of sinful pleasure, which he had for so many years been running with desperate eagerness, now filled him with indignation against himself and the great deceiver, by whom (to use his own phrase) he had been "so wretchedly and scandalously befooled."  This he used often to express in the strongest terms.  Before he left his chamber the next day, the whole frame and disposition of his soul was modeled and changed; so that he became, and continued to the last day of his exemplary and truly Christian life, the very reverse of what he had been before.  Thus, this profligate son was stopped, like Saul of Tarsus, in his course of opposition to the holy Lord Jesus, led captive by the power and grace of his divine and compassionate Redeemer, and so transformed in his feelings, principles, and character, that he now zealously built up the faith which before he destroyed.

This soldier of Jesus Christ now entered with cour-

age and steadiness on his Christian course, and was
much more fervent and spiritual than the generality of
professors.  He used constantly to rise at four in the
morning, and to spend his time till six in the secret
exercises of devotion—reading, meditation, and prayer.
It certainly tended very much to strengthen that faith
in God, and reverent, animating sense of his presence,
for which he was so eminently remarkable.  In all
the trials and services of life, he "endured, as seeing
Him who is invisible."  When a journey or a march
required him to be on horseback by four, he would
be at his devotions by two; and I doubt not but
his uncommon progress in piety was in a great measure owing to these resolute habits of self-denial.  He
early began a practice, which to the last day of his
life he retained—of reproving vice and profaneness,
and was never afraid to debate the matter with any,
under the consciousness of such superiority in the goodness of his cause.

Being for some years out of commission, he resided
in London, where he continued in communication with
the Christian Society, under the pastoral care of Dr.
Calamy.  As his pious mother also belonged to the
same, it must have been an unspeakable pleasure to
her to have frequent opportunities of conversing with
such a son; of observing, in his daily conduct and discourses, the blessed effects of that change which Divine grace had made in his heart; and of sitting down
with him every month at that sacred feast, where Christians so frequently enjoy the divinest entertainments

which they expect on this side heaven.  I the rather
mention this ordinance, because, as this excellent lady
had a very high esteem for it, so she had an opportunity of attending but the very Lord's day immediately
preceding her death, which happened on Thursday,
October 7th, 1725.  He maintained her handsomely
as an affectionate and dutiful son ; and when she expressed her gratitude to him, he 'assured her, that he
esteemed it a great honor, that God put it in his power
to make such a small acknowledgment of all her care
for him, and especially of the many prayers she had
offered on his account, which had already been so remarkably answered, and the benefit of which he hoped
ever to enjoy.  Parents may here see what advantage
it is, even to themselves, to have their children pious,
and what pains they ought to take, by precept, example, prayer, and every other suitable means, to promote
their spiritual welfare, if they wish to •see them kind
and obedient, instead of being, as wicked and neglected
children will be, rebellious, selfish, and ungrateful.
After the removal of his honored parent, this servant
of God still went on his way rejoicing.  On one occasion, he thus writes to an intimate and pious friend :—
" What would I have given this day for paper, pen,
and ink, when the Spirit of the Most High rested upon
me !  O, for the tongue of an angel, to declare what
God hath done this day for my soul !  But it is in vain
to attempt it : all that I am able to say is this, that my
soul has been for some hours joining with the blessed
spirits above in giving ' glory, and honor, and praise,

unto Him that sitteth upon the throne, and to the Lamb, for ever and ever.' My praises began from a renewed view of Him whom I saw pierced for my transgressions. I summoned the whole hierarchy of heaven to join with me; and I am persuaded they all echoed back praises to the Most High. Sure I need not make use of many words to persuade you that are saints to join me in blessing and praising his holy name."

This pious parent, exemplary Christian, and excellent man, was killed at Preston-Pans, in Scotland, September 31st, 1745, leaving an example, both as a saint, and as the head of a family, which I hope every reader of this narrative will, through grace, endeavor to imitate.

---

## DR. DODDRIDGE AND HIS MOTHER.

The celebrated author of "The Family Expositor" was born in London, June 26th, 1702. His father, Daniel Doddridge, was an oilman, resident in London, and the son of one of the ministers ejected by the Act of Uniformity. His mother was the daughter of the Rev. John Beauman, of Prague, in Bohemia, who was compelled to forsake his native country, in consequence of the persecutions which threatened to succeed the expulsion of Frederick, Elector Palatine. Dr. Doddridge was the twentieth and youngest child; all the rest, except one daughter, having died in infancy. It

6*

is not a little singular, that when Doddridge was born, he was laid aside as a dead child; but a person in the room observing some motion in him, took that care of him upon which the flame of life depended. His parents were eminently pious, and his earliest years were by them consecrated to the acquisition of religious knowledge. *The history of the Old and New Testament his mother taught him, before he could read, by means of some Dutch tiles, in the chimney corner of the room where they resided.* He was first sent to school to a Mr. Stott, who instructed him in the rudiments of Greek and Latin; but from this seminary he was removed, when ten years of age, to a Free School, at Kingston-upon-Thames, of which his grandfather, Beauman, had been formerly the master. He remained at that school three years, and was distinguished for his piety and diligence. In 1715 he was deprived by death of his father, and not long afterward of his excellent mother, to whose instructions, under the Divine blessing, he owed his early religious impressions. Of both his parents he always spoke in terms of the warmest affection and respect. In the same year, he was sent to the school of Mr. Nathaniel Wood, of St. Albans, where he commenced his acquaintance with the learned and excellent Mr. Samuel Clark, who not only became to him a wise counselor and an affectionate minister, but a disinterested, generous, and liberal friend and benefactor.

At that school he greatly improved himself in the knowledge of the learned languages, became perfect

master of his native tongue, and accustomed himself
not only to form ideas, but with propriety and elegance
to express them. He devoted much time to reading—
diligently studied history, both civil and ecclesiastical;
and spent a great part of his time in the study of theology. His piety now became more habitual and evident, and on February 1st, 1718, when he was sixteen,
he was admitted a member of the church, under the
pastoral care of Mr. Clark.

In October, 1719, Mr. Clark placed him in the academy of the learned and pious Dr. Jennings, who resided at Knibworth, in Leicestershire. There Dr.
Doddridge greatly improved in every branch of literature, and besides attending to all his academical studies,
he, in one half year, read sixty books, consisting principally of theology, and that not in a hasty and careless
manner, but with great seriousness and advantage.
Though young, cheerful, and devoted to the attainment
of knowledge, he did not, however, forget the more
important concerns of his own personal religion. He
formed some admirable rules for the regulation of his
conduct and the improvement of his time, which he
did not merely form, but cheerfully and invariably
performed. In 1723, his tutor, Mr. Jennings, died,
having not long removed from Knibworth to Hinckley.
Soon after his death, Dr. Doddridge preached his first
sermon at Hinckley, from the words, "If any man
love not the Lord Jesus, let him be anathema marana-
tha;" and two persons ascribed their conversion to the
blessing of God on that sermon. For more than a

year he continued to preach at Hinckley and the neighboring places, when, having received an invitation from the congregation at Knibworth, he accepted their offer, and was there settled in June, 1723.   In that retired and obscure village, there were no external objects to divert his attention from the pursuit of his studies, and his favorite authors; Baxter, Howe, and Tillotson he read with frequency and attention.   To his pastoral duties he was not, however, inattentive; but in religious conversations and visits of mercy he spent a suitable portion of his valuable time.   His preaching was plain and practical; and whilst his mind was richly stored with knowledge, and his imagination was lively, he made all his talents subservient to the moral and religious improvement of the people committed to his care.   During the whole year he accustomed himself to rise every morning at five o'clock, and thus, as he would sometimes say, he had ten years more than he otherwise would have had.

Toward the end of the year (in 1729), he received an invitation to settle at Northampton, in consequence of the removal of Mr. Tingly, the Dissenting minister, to London, and urged by Mr. Some and Mr. Clark to accept the call.   He quitted Harborough, December the 14th, and immediately entered on his more arduous and important duties.   Soon after his settlement, he became seriously ill; but on his recovery in March, 1730, he was set apart to the pastoral office.   In this year he published a tract, entitled, "Free thoughts on the most probable means of reviving religion, occasioned by the late inquiry into the causes of its decay, addressed to the author of that inquiry." That tract was favorably received; and for its spirit and temper deserves much praise. He performed the various duties of a Dissenting pastor with exemplary diligence and affection. His sermons were well studied, and delivered with zeal and affection. He watched over his flock like one who had to give an account. He prayed with and for them. He visited the sick; attended to the wants of the poor; admonished those who erred; cautioned those who wavered; confirmed those who were undecided; and in every respect attended to the doctrines, discipline, and practice of his church and congregation.

Dr. Doddridge sustained all the relationships of life with honor to himself and advantage to his family, and the world; so that as he approached nearer to the eternal world, his path, indeed, resembled that of the just, which is as the shining light that shineth more and more unto the perfect day.

---

## THOMAS COKE, LL.D., AND HIS MOTHER.

THIS pious and useful minister was born at Brecon, in South Wales, on the 9th September, 1747. His father, Mr. Bartholomew Coke, was an eminent surgeon, residing in that place, a man of great respectability, and several times filled the office of chief magistrate of the town. Thomas was their only child, and his affectionate parents watched over his infant days with unusual solicitude. In early life he was, however, deprived by death of his father; and to the care of his widowed mother he was consigned. She was eminently qualified for the charge that devolved on her, and early strove to implant in his youthful mind the seeds of piety and wisdom. She placed him at the college-school at Brecon, where he received the first rudiments of knowledge, and became attentive and studious. At the age of sixteen, he was removed from Brecon to Oxford, and in the Lent term of his seventeenth year was entered a gentleman commoner at Jesus College, in that University. At college he became acquainted with the vicious and profane, and was even a captive to those snares of infidelity which he had at first surveyed with detestation and horror. His principles being thus tainted, his conduct became infected; but he was preserved, to a great degree, from committing those abominable crimes which he observed performed by others. Mr. Coke was, however, unhappy, and amidst all the noise and clamor, and mirth and folly of his associates, he was often pensive and discontented. Doubtless, the remembrance of his widowed mother's pious lessons and instructions clung to his mind, and kept his conscience from sinking into a complete lethargy.

At this time he paid a visit to a clergyman in Wales, and, by the preaching of the Gospel at that place— by perusing the discourses and disputations of Bishop Sherlock—and by reading the celebrated treatise on

Regeneration, by Dr. Witherspoon, his mind became gradually enlightened, though he did not, at that time, become a Christian. On June 17th, 1775, he took his degree of Doctor of Civil Laws; and obtained a curacy at South Petherton, in Somersetshire, where his congregation increased. He built a gallery to the church at his own expense. He evinced great anxiety for the improvement of his charge, and was speedily accused of being a Methodist.

To the doctrines of Mr. Wesley he became attached, zealously preached them at South Petherton, received a reprimand for his zeal from the Bishop of Bath and Wells, and was eventually dismissed by the Rector of the parish for his pious concern to promote the welfare of his parishioners. Banished from the church of South Petherton, he preached in the open air, and attracted considerable attention. In the month of July, 1777, he met with Mr. Wesley, conversed with him, received an explanation of his plans and system, and determined to become a preacher in that society. As a preacher in London, he became very popular, and his fame rapidly spread over an extensive district. In 1780, Mr. Wesley appointed him to superintend the London circuit, and he subsequently visited the various Wesleyan societies in Ireland, and was throughout life distinguished for zeal, ability, and piety. After devoting many years to the establishment of Christian Missions in the West Indies, etc., etc., he died on his passage to India, January 1st, 1814.

## MRS. HANNAH WOODD AND REV. BASIL WOODD.

Mrs. Hannah Woodd was born at Richmond, in Surrey, on the 19th of April, 1736. In July, 1759, she was married to Mr. Basil Woodd, who was also born at Richmond, in 1730, and with whom she had been acquainted from her infancy. Such a union, cemented by long endearment and similarity of disposition, promised a scene of much temporal felicity; but a mysterious dispensation of Divine providence determined it otherwise. The January following, Mr. Woodd, being then from home on a visit, was seized with a violent fever, and died on the 12th of that month. So great a shock, to a mind of her sensibility, could leave no faint impression; but it pleased God to support her in this keen trial, and on the 5th of August following she was delivered of a son. Providence wonderfully interposed in her favor; and both root and branch, though then apparently withering, were preserved together, just as many years longer as she had then lived.

The afflictive circumstance of her husband's death, nevertheless, proved an eventual blessing, though conveyed in the disguise of woe. By one stroke her mind was severed from worldly prospects, and being rent from the love of the creature, she now began more anxiously to seek the knowledge and love of the Creator. She had from early life been of a devout turn of mind, a strict observer of moral duties, and the ritual of religion; but now, in the day of adversity, she was

brought to deeper views of the depravity of her heart,
and the need she stood in of a Saviour.  She perceived
the insufficiency of her own righteousness, and the necessity of being born again.

Pious friends who had sympathized in her late affliction, now observing the spiritual concern of her
mind, availed themselves of this opportunity to bring
her under the ministry of the Gospel.   Amongst these
were principally Mrs. Conyers, and Mrs. Wilberforce,
with whom her acquaintance had commenced at school,
and by whom she was about this time introduced to
the acquaintance of Dr. Conyers, and the Rev. Mr.
Venn.  In the spirit of true Christian friendship, they
lamented that she had hitherto had no better instruction than mere moral essays, and brought her acquainted with sound evangelical principles.   These proved
indeed the spiritual food which her soul hungered after :
she received them in faith and love, adored them in
her life, and found them her triumph in her dying hour.
From this happy period, to a disposition naturally be-
nign and amiable, were added the graces of the Holy
Spirit ; and the Christian motive of love to the Lord
Jesus, gave life and spirituality to her moral duties.
Religious exercises, which hitherto she had not regarded higher than as a devout form of godliness, now became her soul's delight.  She ordinarily retired three
times in the day for private prayer ; at morning, noon,
and at evening.   Love to God her Saviour, led her
with cheerful feet to the courts of the Lord's house—
a privilege she so highly valued, that she rarely per-
7

mitted inclement weather or the decay of her health to interfere with it.

Though filial affection may be suspected of exaggerating a mother's excellence, yet it is but justice to say that in every department she was a lovely ornament of the truth as it is in Jesus; particularly as a daughter, a mother, and a mistress. As to the former relation— she constantly attended her father till his death, at the advanced age of eighty-seven, who, though he was very much prejudiced against her religious principles, yet lived to have his mind greatly won by her uniform conduct; and on his death-bed he regretted that he had ever opposed her, and acknowledged in the most affecting manner, his long experience of her filial duty.

As a mother, the Rev. Dr. Conyers frequently said, "That he never saw such an instance of maternal affection." Her son says, "This is a subject on which, I hope, I shall never think without heartfelt gratitude to her and to God, who so favored me. The whole of her deportment was calculated to win my early attention to religion. I saw in her what it could do:—How happy! how cheerful! how humble! how holy! how lovely in life, and afterward in death! how full of mercy and good fruits, it could render the happy possessor! As I was the only son of my mother, and she a widow, she might perhaps lean to the side of over-indulgence. Yet, if my heart do not deceive me, in trusting that I love the ways of God—I am indebted, through Divine grace, for that inestimable benefit, to the impression of her great and tender kindness, her uniform example, and particularly her pious and affectionate letters, when I was about thirteen years old. Such, indeed, has been the impression of her parental affections, that though my friends, I believe, have never charged me with filial negligence, yet since her decease, I have regretted very frequently, that in many little instances, I conceive I might have shown her still more respect and affection."

Evidences of the joyful state of her mind may be collected from what she said on her death-bed. On her son's return from St. Peter's, Cornhill, that evening, she took hold of his hand and seemed much animated. " God," said she, " my dear, has been very gracious this afternoon: he sent my son from me, but he sent Himself to me. O, I am very happy! I am going to my mansion in the skies. I shall soon be there ; and oh, I shall be glad to receive you to it. You shall come in, but you shall never go out—no, never !" Pausing a little, she said : " If ever you have a family, tell the children they had a grandmother who feared God, and found the comforts of it on her death-bed. And tell your partner I shall be glad to see her in heaven ; when you come to glory, you must bring her with you. Let me tell you by my own experience, when you come to lie upon your death-bed, an interest in Jesus will be found a precious possession. O ! what a mercy of mercies that we should be brought out of the bondage of Egypt, and united together in the kingdom of God's dear Son ! I exhort you to preach the Gospel ; preach it faithfully and boldly. Fear not the face of man.

Endeavor to put in a word of comfort to the humble believer—to poor weak souls. I heartily wish you success :—may you be useful to the souls of many !" At another time, she said, addressing her son : " God has greatly indulged my desires ; has answered my prayers in a wonderful manner. How has he dealt with me in sparing me so long to see you, my son, settled in life ! I remember, when I used to express my anxiety for your eternal welfare to a friend of mine, he always said —in allusion to the story of Monica, the mother of St. Augustine—' Go home and make yourself easy—the child of those tears can never perish.' Now, my dear, when God has removed me, imitate St. Augustine's behavior after the death of Monica ; do not be dejected ; think of the happiness I shall then be enjoying, and say as he said, when some wondered at his cheerfulness, ' My mother is not a woman to be lamented.' " She expired on the 12th of November, 1784.

## SIR WILLIAM JONES AND HIS MOTHER.

This learned and distinguished man was born in London, on the eve of St. Michael, in the year 1746. Mr. Jones, his father, survived the birth of his son William but three years : his family was respectable, and his character excellent. The care of the education of William now devolved upon his mother, who, in many respects, was eminently qualified for the task. She had by nature a strong understanding, which was improved by his conversation and instruction. Under the tuition of her husband, she became a considerable proficient in Algebra, and with a view to qualify herself for the office of preceptor to her sister's son, who was destined to a maritime profession, made herself perfect in Trigonometry and the theory of Navigation. Mrs. Jones, after the death of her husband, was urgently and repeatedly solicited by the Countess of Macclesfield to remain at Sherborn Castle; but having formed a plan for the education of her son, with an unalterable determination to pursue it, and being apprehensive that her residence at Sherborn might interfere with the execution of it, she declined accepting the friendly invitation of the Countess, who never ceased to retain the most affectionate regard for her. In the plan adopted by Mrs. Jones for the instruction of her son, she proposed to reject the severity of discipline, and to lead his mind insensibly to knowledge and exertion, by exciting his curiosity and directing it to useful objects.

She so cultivated his mind, that at four years of age he was able to read any English book, and until his eighth or ninth year, she was his only preceptor. When in his ninth year he had the misfortune to break his thigh bone, which detained him at home more than a year; his mother was his constant companion, and amused him daily by the perusal of such English books as were adapted to his taste and capacity. To his incessant importunities for information she was in the habit of using one reply, which from his earliest years made a due impression on him. This remark was, *"read and*

7*

*you will know.*" At a subsequent period of his life, Sir William Jones was in the habit of saying, that he owed all his intellectual improvement to his early obedience to his mother's favorite maxim—"*read and you will know.*"

With regard to religious instruction, she early taught him the creed and the ten commandments, but one effect of her daily maxim is too remarkable to be passed over in silence. One morning, as he was turning over the leaves of a Bible in his mother's closet, his attention was forcibly arrested by the sublime description of the angel, in the tenth chapter of Revelation; and the impression which his mind received was never after erased. At a period of mature judgment, he considered the passage as equal in sublimity to any of the inspired writings, and far superior to any that could be produced from mere human compositions; and he was fond of relating and mentioning the rapture which he felt when he first read it. This remarkable incident took place before he had completed his fifth year.

His spiritual attainments as a Christian were quite worthy of his learning and literary distinction. In his mature years, when he had secured enduring fame and worldly honors, he says : " I have carefully and regularly perused the Holy Scriptures, and am of opinion, that the volume called the Bible, independent of its divine origin, contains more sublimity, purer morality, more important history, and finer strains of eloquence, than can be collected from all other books, in whatever language they may have been written."

## LADY WILHELMINA MAXWELL GLENORCHY AND HER MOTHER.

This lady was distinguished during the last century for her benevolence and piety. She was born at Preston, in North Britain, in the year 1742. She was the daughter of Dr. Wm. Maxwell, a gentleman of great fortune and respectability, also residing at Preston. Four months previous to her birth, Dr. Maxwell died; and on her excellent and amiable mother, afterward Lady Alva, devolved the task of educating her daughter. The instructions she received were such as to improve the heart, as well as to enlighten the understanding. Her mind was strong and vigorous, yet polished and delicate. Her memory was retentive—her person interesting—her behavior affable — her imagination lively, and her temper excellent. Her juvenile years, though sedulously watched over by her kind, intelligent mother, were, nevertheless, too much devoted to the follies and gayety of fashionable life. When, however, she had attained the age of twenty-three years, her mind was aroused, by a serious illness, to reflections on her present character and future prospects; and musing on the first questions in the Assembly's Catechism: "What is the chief end of man?" "It is to glorify God and enjoy him forever." She asked herself, "Have I answered the design of my being? Have I glorified God? And shall I enjoy him forever?" Thus reflecting, she gradually felt the sinfulness of her nature; perceived the total alienation of her heart from God;

and applied to her heavenly Father for pardon and grace. Like many young professors of religion, she endeavored at first to conceal from observation, the change which had been wrought in her heart, and, as far as possible, to compromise with the world, but such conduct she soon discovered to be incompatible with spirituality of mind; and she therefore determined on making an open and decided profession of Christianity. She employed much of her time in acts of benevolence, in wise and pious conversation, in an extensive, judicious, and profitable correspondence, and in every other means, for promoting the conversion of sinners, and the edification of saints. She expended much money in printing and circulating religious tracts, and at her desire and expense was composed and published a *Gaelic translation* of Allein's "Alarm to the Unconverted," which has been productive of much good in the Highlands.

She devoted large sums of money in placing the families of religious individuals in situations of comfort. She paid great attention to the religious instruction of the poor, and, in consequence of such instruction, very many became useful members of society. In Edinburgh, she erected a large chapel, and added to it a Free-school, for teaching reading, writing, and arithmetic, which she liberally endowed. She also erected and endowed at Strathfillan, on the estate of Lord Breadalbane,—and her executrix, by her desire, erected at Hotwells, near Bristol, a neat and commodious chapel. Aware of the importance of attending to the preparation of young men for the work of the ministry, she generously encouraged that important object; assisted many poor congregations in paying the salaries of their ministers, and in otherwise supporting religious worship. For such benevolent actions, the worldly and irreligious branded her with the name of Methodist, and endeavored to represent her as a wild enthusiast; but such opposition to her principles enabled her patiently to endure, and through evil and good report, to pursue her work of faith and labor of love. She was attached to the principles of the Church of England, but more highly approved of the preachers, and mode of worship belonging to, and adopted by, the Countess of Huntingdon. Her incessant and varied occupations appear to have injured her health; and she had scarcely attained to years of maturity, when the world and the church were deprived of this friend to humanity and religion. Her temper was warm, and she sometimes appeared to entertain too high an opinion of her own importance, but her virtues and graces were so pre-eminent, that her imperfections were unobserved or forgotten. Though her health declined, her activity and usefulness were unabated, till on the 17th of July, 1786, she was summoned to receive that reward, which on every diligent and faithful servant, God has promised to bestow. She bequeathed by her will £5000 for the education of young men for the ministry in England; £5000 to the society in Scotland, for the propagation of Christian knowledge, and the greatest part of the residue of her property to charitable and pious purposes.

### REV. E. D. JACKSON AND HIS MOTHER.

EDWARD DUNCAN JACKSON was descended from a very respectable family. He appears from his infancy to have been of an inquisitive, reasoning, and solid turn. While yet a little child, he was impressed with veneration for the Deity, and attachment to his worship. At a very early age, he constantly attended Divine service twice a day, at St. George's Church in the Borough, taking a prayer-book with him, and conducting himself as orderly as if attained to mature age and understanding. At four years old, he went one Sacrament Sabbath by himself; but instead of leaving with the congregation, he remained with the communicants, to the no small alarm of his mother, who, making ineffectual inquiry for him, concluded he was stolen. From this fear she was relieved by his return with the beadle, who stated, that at the earnest solicitation of the child, the minister was prevailed on to allow him to be present; that he went to the table with the communicants; and kneeling with them, partook of the bread; but was omitted in the handing of the wine; "because," said little Jackson to his mother, "by being so small, I was overlooked by the clergyman."

At this period, he was accustomed to bring home and repeat the text, and parts of the discourse; and would be very frequent and fervent in private prayer. Before he was six years old, he gave a very striking, though child-like, evidence of his conviction of the omniscience of God.   Playing in a field, he lost one of his shoe-buckles, which, being silver, distressed him much ; on which, he immediately retired to a corner of the field, and kneeling down, prayed to God with great earnestness, that he might be directed to it.   About the same time, he had also convictions of sin, and rea- soned much about the plan of salvation.   His serious inquiries and impressions, *cherished by a pious parent*, excited the fond hope of seeing another Timothy, fear- ing God from his youth ; but the apostolic remark was soon verified, " Evil communications corrupt good man- ners."   Mingling with wicked boys and profane work- men, he lost his youthful piety, frequently broke the Sabbath, attended the theatre, and delighted in vain and sinful amusements.   Thus, the plant, which prom- ised to be so fair and fruitful, soon began to shed its fading leaves.   Twice, during this period, he was won- derfully rescued from a watery grave ; but these de- liverances, and other innumerable mercies, left no de- vout or lasting impression upon his mind.   At length, in his sixteenth year, as he was pursuing his pleasures one Lord's day, seeing the people go into church, where the Rev. Mr. Foster was preaching, he went in with them, and was seriously affected by the discourse. This happily proved the beginning of a work of recov- ering grace.   Continuing his attendance upon the or- dinances of religion, he was brought to feel his guilty and perishing state, and led humbly to seek salvation through the atonement made by our Redeemer.   Old things now passed away, and in Christ Jesus he became a new creature. He was soon afterward directed to the acquaintance of a "mother in Israel," whose heart and house were open to the people of God. To her he frequently resorted, and derived much benefit from her judicious counsels. On one of these occasions, she insisted upon his praying with her. The good old lady next persuaded him to engage in a select company, who assembled at her house for prayer and exhortation. With this society he met constantly, sometimes praying, but never attempting to speak, till one evening, when, being disappointed of their speaker, the venerable matron fixed upon Mr. Jackson to supply the lack of service. A call so public and unexpected overwhelmed him for a time; but all waiting in silence, and every eye being fixed upon him, he felt the attempt a duty, and entreating the Lord for assistance, he addressed them in such a way as left no hesitation on the mind of any present respecting his fitness for the work of the ministry. He was now about eighteen, and continued to preach in London and its environs till the expiration of his apprenticeship. He afterward visited Worcester, Bristol, and other places, in all of which his labors have been successful; and November 9th, 1793, he was ordained to the pastoral office at Warminster in Wiltshire, being then in the 24th year of his age. The church and congregation increased under his care; but his studies, labors, and trials, impaired his constitution, and in June, 1803, he was seized with dizziness and faintings, and obliged, though with great reluctance, to lay aside his beloved work. He lingered for several months in a state of painful debility, which, in September, was succeeded by vomiting and convulsions, making it evident that death was at hand.

One of his friends, asking him in that solemn hour what were his views of the Gospel, he answered—

> "Firm as the earth Thy Gospel stands,
>     My Lord, my hope, my trust ;
> If I am found in Jesu's hands,
>     My soul can ne'er be lost."

The grief of his beloved and sorrowing partner much agitated his mind : he could only say, as she was carried out of his room, "My dear Mary, I commit you to the care of a covenant God."  To a relative he said, "I have always loved you; be kind to my wife and children.  Good night—good night forever !"  One of his deacons, inquiring if he preferred any text from which his death might be improved to his people, he said—"No ;" but pausing a moment, added—"except that which has been my living doctrine, and is now my dying hope : ' It is a faithful saying, and worthy of all acceptation, that Jesus Christ came into the world to save sinners, of whom I am chief ;' give my love to the Church. and say that I wish them a better and more faithful pastor."

Thus full of faith, humility, patience, and love, entered into the presence of his Lord.

8

## ROBERT BLOOMFIELD AND HIS MOTHER.

ROBERT was the youngest child of George Bloomfield, a tailor, at Honington. His father died when he was an infant under a year old. His mother was a school-mistress, and instructed her own children with the others. He thus learned to read as soon as he learned to speak. Though the mother was left a widow with six small children, yet, with the help of friends, she managed to give each of them a little schooling.

Robert was accordingly sent to Mr. Rodwell, of Ix-worth, to be improved in writing; but he did not go to that school more than two or three months, nor was ever sent to any other: his mother again marrying when Robert was about seven years old. By her second husband, John Glover, she had another family.

When Robert was not above eleven years old, the late Mr. W. Austin, of Sapiston, took him. And though it is customary for farmers to pay such boys only one and sixpence per week, yet he generously took him into the house. This relieved his mother of any other expense, than only of finding him a few things to wear, and this was more than she well knew how to do. She wrote, therefore, Mr. G. Bloomfield continues, to me and my brother Nat (then in London), to assist her—mentioning that he, Robert, was so small of his age, that Mr. Austin said, "he was not likely to get his living by hard labor."

Mr. G. Bloomfield, on this, informed his mother that

if she would let him take the boy with him, he would take him and teach him to make shoes, and Nat promised to clothe him.   The mother, upon this offer, took coach and came to London to Mr. G. Bloomfield, with the boy, for she said, " she never should have been happy if she had not put him herself into his hands." She charged me, he adds, *"as I valued a mother's blessing, to watch over him, to set good examples before him, and never to forget that he had lost his father."* I religiously confine myself to Mr. G. Bloomfield's own words, and think I should wrong all the parties concerned, if, in mentioning this pathetic and successful admonition, I were to use any other.

It was while working at his trade as a shoemaker, and engaged in running errands for the other workmen, that the youth commenced composing poetry. As he had not the opportunity of using writing implements, and probably was often unable to procure them, his method was to compose mentally, and retain the verses in his memory until a favorable opportunity occurred for committing them to paper.   His first effusions were sent off anonymously to the weekly newspaper which his brother and the other workmen took in.   Great must have been the joy of the boy, to find the little poems thus sent, obtained insertion in " the Poet's Corner " of the paper.   At first, he had not courage to own himself the author, but was both elated and amused at the praises he heard bestowed on the anonymous lines, by the shoemakers.

The first poem that brought him into note, was " The

Farmer's Boy," which he composed in the manner above related, putting down long portions of the poem at favorable intervals of his daily toil.   The beauty of this poem, its exquisite descriptions of country scenery, manners, pursuits, and objects, soon rendered it a favorite, and Bloomfield began to obtain celebrity, which he afterward increased by the publication of his "Wild Flowers," and " Rural Tales."

Through life he was a poor man, but his genius obtained him many devoted admirers; and his name will ever rank high amid the uneducated poets of England. To the close of his life, his mother's name never passed his lips without eliciting sentiments of affection and reverence for her memory.

----

## REV. JOHN NEWTON AND HIS MOTHER.

### SEED EARLY SOWN.

He says—"I was born in London, July 24th, 1725. My parents, though not wealthy, were respectable. My father was many years master of a ship in the Mediterranean trade.   My mother was a Dissenter, a pious woman, and a member of the late Dr. Jennings' church.   She was of a weak, consumptive habit; loved retirement; and as I was her only child, she made it the chief business and pleasure of her life to instruct me, and bring me up 'in the nurture and admonition of the Lord.'   I have been told that from my birth she had, in her mind, devoted me to the ministry; and that had she lived till I was of a proper age, I was to have been sent to St. Andrew's, in Scotland, to be educated. But the Lord had appointed otherwise. My mother died before I was seven years of age. I was rather of a sedentary turn, not active and playful, as boys commonly are, but seemed as willing to learn, as my mother was to teach me. When I was four years old, I could read (hard words excepted) as well as I can now; and could likewise repeat the answers to the questions in the ' Assembly's Shorter Catechism,' with the proofs; and all Dr. Watts' smaller catechisms, with his children's hymns." His excellent mother likewise stored his memory with whole chapters and smaller portions of Scripture, and often commended him, with many prayers and tears, to God.

After her death, these hopeful beginnings were apparently lost. His father was too stern, and kept him in a state of fear and bondage. His distance and severity greatly lessened his parental influence, and powerfully inclined the youth to break the yoke of early discipline, and to forsake the ways of God. During this period of his life, up to his fifteenth year, he was often visited by religious convictions; and being, from a child, fond of reading, he met with " Bennet's Christian Oratory," and though he understood little of it, the course of life it recommended appeared very desirable. He therefore began to pray, to read the Scriptures, to keep a diary, and thought himself religious; but soon became weary of it, and gave it up. He then learned to curse and blaspheme, and when out of the view of

8*

his father and step-mother, ran greedily on in the paths of iniquity.  Being exposed at times to imminent danger, he trembled at the idea of appearing in his guilty state before a just and holy God; and often indulged remorse, made vows of obedience, and changed his outward conduct; but returning temptations overcame him again and again.  At length being impressed, and obliged to serve on board a man-of-war, he fell into evil company, and particularly into the society of one who was an expert, a zealous, and plausible infidel. By objections and arguments, young Newton's depraved heart was soon gained.  He plunged into infidelity with all his spirit; and, like an unwary sailor who quits the harbor just before a rising storm, the hopes and comforts of the Gospel were renounced at the very time when every other comfort was about to fail.  This prodigal son now entered on a scene of guilt, danger, and misery which has seldom been exceeded; but a kind Providence visibly watched over him, and at length it pleased God to make him a vessel of his mercy, and a minister of his grace.  March 21st, 1748, the ship in which he was returning to England being in the most imminent danger, a deep and abiding impression was made upon his mind.  "On that day," to use his own words, "the Lord sent from on high and delivered me out of deep waters.  I continued at the pump from three in the morning till near noon, and then I could do no more.  I went and lay down upon my bed, uncertain, and almost indifferent, whether I should rise again.  In an hour's time I was called; and not being able to pump, I went to the helm, and steered the ship till midnight, excepting a small interval for refreshment. I had here leisure and convenient opportunity for reflection. I began to think of my former religious professions; the extraordinary turns of my life; the calls, warnings, and deliverances I had met with; the licentious course of my conversation; particularly my unparalleled effrontery in making the Gospel history the constant subject of profane ridicule. I thought there never was, or could be, such a sinner as myself; and then comparing the advantages I had broken through, I concluded, at first, that my sins were too great to be forgiven. The Scripture, likewise, seemed to say the same; for I had formerly been well acquainted with the Bible, and many passages, upon this occasion, returned upon my memory; particularly those awful passages—Proverbs i. 24–31; Hebrews vi. 4–6; 2 Peter ii. 20; which seemed so exactly to suit my case and character, as to bring with them a presumptive proof of a Divine original. When I saw, beyond all probability, that there was still hope of respite, and heard, about six in the evening, that the ship was freed from water, there arose a gleam of hope. I thought I saw the hand of God displayed in our favor. I began to pray; I could not utter the prayer of faith; I could not draw near to a reconciled God, and call him 'Father;' my prayer was like the cry of the ravens, which yet the Lord does not disdain to hear. I now began to think of that Jesus whom I had so often derided; I recollected the particulars of his life, and of his death; a death for sins not his own, but, as I remembered, for the sake of those who, in their distress, should put their trust in him. One of the first helps I received, in consequence of a determination to examine the New Testament more carefully, was from Luke xi. 13, ' If ye then being evil, know how to give good gifts unto your children; how much more shall your Heavenly Father give the Holy Spirit to them that ask Him?' Here I found a *spirit* spoken of who was to be communicated to those who ask it. Upon this I reasoned thus—if this book be true, the promise in this passage must be true likewise. I have need of that very Spirit, by which the whole was written, to understand it aright. He has engaged here to give that Spirit to those who ask; I must, therefore, pray for it; and, if it be of God, he will make good his own word. My purposes were strengthened by John vii. 17."

Their danger of shipwreck was not yet passed, but rather became more imminent than before. However, at a time when they were ready to give up all for lost, and despair appeared in every countenance, they began to conceive hope from the winds shifting to the desired point, so as best to suit that broken part of the ship, which must be kept out of the water, and so gently to blow as their few remaining sails could bear.

On the 19th of April, they anchored in Lough Swilly, Ireland. When they came into this port, their very last victuals were boiling in the pot, and before they had been there two hours, the wind—which seem-

ed to have been providentially restrained till they were
in a place of safety,—began to blow with great violence; so that, if they had continued at sea that night,
they must, in all human estimation, have gone to the
bottom. "About this time," says Mr. Newton, "I
began to know that there is a God who hears and
answers prayers." Speaking of the ship in which he
lately sailed, he says,—"There were no persons on
board to whom I could open myself with freedom
concerning the state of my soul; none from whom I
could ask advice. As to books, I had a New Testament, Stanhope's Thomas-a-Kempis, and a volume of
Bishop Beveridge's Sermons, one of which, upon our
Lord's passion, affected me much. In perusing the
New Testament, I was struck with several passages,
particularly that of the fig-tree, Luke xiii.; the case of
Paul, 1 Timothy i.; but above all, that of the prodigal, Luke xv. I thought that it had never been so
nearly exemplified as by myself; and then the goodness of the father in receiving, nay, in running to meet
such a son, and this intended only to illustrate the
Lord's goodness to returning sinners! Such reflections gaining upon me, I continued much in prayer.
Outward circumstances helped, in this place, to make
me still more serious and earnest in crying to Him
who alone could relieve me; and sometimes I thought
I could be content to die, even for want of food, so I
might but die a believer."

The spiritual change, thus happily begun, was evi-
dently from above. Mr. Newton became an exemplary

and devoted Christian, and was ordained by the Bishop of Lincoln, in 1764. For more than forty years he approved himself a faithful, judicious, and affectionate minister of Christ. The benevolence of his disposition, and the piety of his heart, will appear from his own words,—": I see in this world two heaps, of human happiness and misery : now, if I can take but the smallest bit from one heap and add to the other, I carry a point. If, as I go home, a child has dropped a halfpenny, and if, by giving it another, I can wipe away its tears, I feel I have done something. I should be glad, indeed, to do greater things, but I will not neglect this. When I hear a knock at my study door, I hear a message from God. It may be a lesson of instruction; perhaps, a lesson of patience; but since it is *His* message, it must be interesting." His house was open to Christians of all ranks and denominations. Here, like a father among his children, he used to entertain, encourage, and instruct his friends; especially younger ministers, or candidates for the ministry. Here, also, the poor, the afflicted, and the tempted found an asylum and a sympathy, which they could scarcely find in an equal degree anywhere besides. Not having any children of his own, he had no opportunity of discharging the duties of a parent; but he adopted two nieces into his family, toward whom he displayed the wisdom and affection of a pious father; while they, in return, loved and reverenced him as daughters.

My pen would still linger while portraying a char-

acter so venerable and interesting; but I must forbear.
I therefore only add, that Mr. Newton died in peace,
December 21st, 1807, in the eighty-second year of his
age. *Behold, in his example, the efficacy of Christian
instruction and prayer, even at a very early period.*
His pious mother died before he was seven years of
age. Yet, she sowed "precious seed," with weeping
and supplication, in the mind of her son, which, though
it appeared to be choked for a time, brought forth at
length a rich and valuable harvest. She devoted him,
in humility and faith, to the ministry; and though for
a season he seemed of all men most unlikely and unfit
for the sacred office, yet God by his grace prepared
him for it, made him a "burning and a shining light,"
and enabled him successfully to build up the faith
which once he labored to destroy. Perhaps he might
never have wandered into the paths of irreligion, had
his father been pious, judicious, tender, and patient,
like his mother. It is highly important that both parents should unite in the spiritual care of their children; that they may see their comfort and usefulness
through life, and at last, present them with joy before
the God and Father of all.

---

## MRS. CHASE AND HER CHILDREN.

She writes thus concerning her youth—"Having had
a pious education, it taught me to reverence the Sabbath, and though it could not give me a love to the

day, yet it led me to read books that were suitable to the day ; which was one of the means the Lord made use of to set me thinking about the concerns of my immortal soul.  I used to inquire of myself, when it was that God would take an account of the actions of a child, and hoped that I was not old enough ; but still, I rather thought or feared I was.  I read the Scriptures, not so much because I understood them, as because I thought there might come a time when I should ; and then, it would be of use to me to be acquainted with them."

These beginnings of serious reflection and desire led, through grace, to her conversion and eminent piety. She entered into the marriage state in April, 1786, and in August, 1789, was left a bereaved widow with three children.  Divine grace supported her under the loss of a pious and amiable husband.  On this affecting occasion, she says, " Never did I see the realities of the invisible world so much as in the trying moments I have lately experienced.  I felt no tremor at depositing the remains of my dear departed husband, because I believe that those who sleep in Jesus, will God bring with him ; and in the meantime he is infinitely happier in the presence of the ever adorable Jesus, than I, or all the world besides, could have made him ; and it is but a little while, and then I shall be where he is, and we shall join in nobler worship than we ever have done here below.  I have been thinking of the important charge the Lord hath committed to me in respect to the children, and these words came to my mind, 'Be faithful over a few things, and I will make thee ruler over many things.'"

After this, Mrs. Chase's grand concern was to train up her children in the fear of God; and taking a few young ladies to educate with them, she endeavored to promote their spiritual and eternal welfare. In the spring of 1798, her health rapidly declined, so that death seemed to be drawing near. On the 10th of March she desired that she might see her children and all her pupils together, in order to give them her last advice. When they were come into her room, she addressed them in the most affectionate manner—"My dear children, I have sent for you to talk to you, as I have not long to be with you. While I was able, it was my greatest delight to instruct you, particularly in the things of God; and I have always loved you with the tenderness of a mother. I earnestly entreat you, my dear children, to seek an interest in Jesus. Search the Scriptures, for they testify of him:" with more to the same purpose. Seeing them in tears, she said, "God bless you all, my dears; and do not grieve. Come now, my dear children, and kiss me for the last time." On the Sabbath, being told that her daughter Eliza had repeated those words, "It is the Lord, let him do what seemeth him good," she expressed great delight that the Lord had subdued her will to his will; as the dear child had previously expressed herself, almost in anger, that the Lord would not hear her prayers and restore her dear mamma.

On Monday, she spoke again to her beloved children,

telling them, she hoped to have lived to see them grow up in the fear of God ; but the Lord had chosen greater happiness for her. She earnestly entreated them to seek Jesus Christ, for salvation. She told them, that from a child, the Scriptures had been her delight. She said the salvation of their souls had always lain near her heart. When they wept, she begged them not to grieve too much, for she should soon be in glory ; and if they loved the Lord Jesus Christ, and trusted in him for salvation, they should all meet again before his throne. She requested them to look upon those relations as parents to whose affection and care she had entrusted them, and to obey them as such,—to behave toward them as they had done to her. Then, turning to her son, she said—" Remember the advice of Solomon : ' My son, if sinners entice thee, consent thou not.' "

On Tuesday evening she gave them her last blessing, saying to each one of them, in a most solemn and affectionate manner—" God the Father, God the Son, and God the Holy Ghost, bless you !" After the children were gone to bed, she begged her sisters to give her up to God in prayer. A few hours before her departure, Mr. P—— prayed with her. On his taking leave, she desired her love to Mrs. P——, wishing them both as happy as she then was; for no greater happiness could she wish them here below. To some Christian friends who called shortly after, she said— " It is comfortable dying with Christ." She often repeated, " I long to be with him." Her last words were—"I am going home," when, heaving a gentle sigh, her wish was accomplished, and she found herself before the Heavenly throne.

---

## MRS. ROBINSON AND HER MOTHER.
### OF THE ISLAND OF GURNSEY.[1]

Mrs. Robinson was born at Dundee, in Scotland, August 27th, 1749. In the seventh year of her age, the instructions of her pious mother, and the good counsels of a Christian friend, led her seriously to inquire, "What must I do to be saved?" In reading the sacred Scriptures, especially those parts of them which describe the sufferings of Christ, she was deeply affected. When she was twelve years of age, she became more decided in favor of religion, and resolved never to rest until she found that peace of God "which passeth all understanding." Satan now perplexed her mind with doubts, and brought her into great distress. Had she consulted her minister, or some pious and judicious friend, she might have obtained an early deliverance. In this unhappy state she continued eighteen months, till at length she opened her mind to her *mother*. Anxious to see her daughter brought into the liberty of the Gospel, this excellent parent united with a few serious persons in fervent prayer to God, and never ceased to intercede with him in her behalf till the dark cloud was dispersed, and divine light began to shine upon her

[1] By the Rev. Wm. Toase.

mind.  By a powerful application of the words of the
prophet, "Seek ye the Lord while he may be found,
call ye upon him while he is near," she was much encouraged to persevere in prayer.  Her soul was soon
filled with joy and peace in believing, and she saw and
felt that Christ was mighty to save.  For some years
after this, she went on her way rejoicing ; but an un-
guarded step, which she took in forming a matrimonial
engagement, was a source of grief to her parents, and
brought darkness and condemnation upon her own
mind.  When adverting to this circumstance in future
life, she often expressed her deep regret.  In the year
1774, she accompanied her husband, who was in the
army, to America, and on June 4th, landed safe at
Boston.  The prayers and conversations of a black
man were made a blessing to her, and she experienced
a revival of religion in her soul.  "At length," she
says, "the fatal day of battle arrived.  Then it was
that I began to think of my disobedience to my parents, and of my departure from God.  A succession
of domestic afflictions added to my distress.  In the
course of one week, my two children were taken ill
and died."  At length she received the heart-rending
news that her husband was no more—he fell in the
contest.  On this mournful occasion, she writes—"Seeing myself a widow, with a fatherless child, in a strange
country, I was ready to abandon myself to despair.
When the letter came to hand, I was on board a trans-
port-ship, ready to sail for New York.  We put to
sea, and after six weeks of tremendous weather, during

which I experienced many hardships, I landed at the place of my destination, on Christmas eve. That was indeed an awful moment. My infant in my arms—not knowing an individual in the place—I knew not what to do; and yielding to a momentary despair of ever finding the peace of mind which I had lost, I came to the desperate resolution of leaping, with my child, into the ebbing tide." This was a day of fearful extremity; but the wings of Providence were spread over this child of many prayers. Just when she was ready to give up all for lost, deliverance was at hand. A sentinel, who was walking on the wharf, seeing she was in distress, went up to her, and caused her baggage to be taken, with herself and child, to a neighboring house, where she found an affectionate and comfortable reception. " I was saved," she gratefully observes, " from temporal and eternal ruin. All my wants were amply supplied. Finding my health much impaired, I began to feel a dread of death; this led me to fervent prayer, and I spent whole nights in wrestling with God, beseeching him once more to cause his face to shine upon me: yet I found no rest to my troubled conscience. On the 1st of August, 1777, we were visited with an awful thunder-storm, at four o'clock in the afternoon: a ship-of-war blew up in the roads, and much damage was done in the city. My child, at that instant, waking out of his sleep, was seized with convulsions, and expired on the following day, at the same hour. O, what I felt, when I considered that God had taken the innocent and spared the guilty!"

9*

After passing through various and trying scenes, and experiencing many proofs of Almighty care and protection, Mrs. Robinson, in the year 1782, had an opportunity of visiting her parents, who received her with joy, exclaiming, " The dead is alive, the lost is found." Her mother said, " Now my prayer is answered in your behalf;" and five weeks after, she departed in peace and in the triumph of faith. Her last words to her daughter were, " I have counseled you, I have prayed for you, I have set you the best example I could ; and now, if you are not found at the right hand of God at the last day, I shall be a witness against you." This dying charge made a deep impression on the mind of Mrs. Robinson, which she never lost.

On May 15th, 1795, she arrived in Guernsey. Here, after much deliberation, she united herself to the Methodists ; and for twenty-nine years, she was deservedly revered and loved, as a " mother in Israel." Many who were unconnected with the society, looked up to her with great respect, and continued to visit her for the benefit of her religious conversation and spiritual advice, as long as her strength permitted her to see them. She was, besides, the faithful and affectionate leader of three large classes, watching over her members as one who must give an account. Her afflictions were heavy for several months before her death ; yet no expression was ever heard to escape her lips contrary to the most perfect resignation. On one occasion she said, " My sufferings are very great, but I am in good hands, and have no anxiety as to the issue ; all this must end well." At another time, " I am willing that my heavenly Father should heat this furnace as hot, and keep me in it as long as he pleaseth : I would not have my own will—His will be done." A little before her death she said, " In the midst of this extreme weakness and pain, I am favored with some most precious intimations of my heavenly Father's love. Heaven is worth suffering for—it is worth dying for." She died in the enjoyment of that perfect love which casteth out fear. The last words she was heard to utter were—" I am happy : I wish all the world felt as I do." She was released from mortality January 16th, 1825.

---

## OBERLIN AND HIS MOTHER.

THE history of modern times furnishes few names more illustrious in the annals of benevolence and philanthropy, than that of John Frederic Oberlin. This pious and admirable man was a native of Strasbourg, and was distinguished from his earliest years for the possession of a generous, tender, and conscientious spirit. While a very young man, he devoted himself to God, was engaged in the work of the ministry among the Protestants of the north-western districts of France, and received the pastoral charge of the people residing in a wild, barren, rocky district—called the Ban de la Roche. This charge called for the exercise of unwearied self-denial, and untiring benevolence. His people, when he first labored among them, were rude, ignorant, and miserable.   Oberlin, for their sakes, and in performance of his Christian duties, gave up all prospects of a more elevated station, and set himself to benefit them by giving them instruction in various useful pursuits, while their spiritual and mental training was the object of his continued solicitude.   Ardently devoting himself to this work of bettering the condition of his people, he made a road, and constructed a bridge that connected their bleak mountains and rocky valleys with the city of Strasbourg—by this means, increasing the traffic of the district.   Besides this, he built schools, erected comfortable cottages, founded libraries, set up a printing-press, made extensive plantations, and by his agricultural skill, changed the appearance of the whole country, and introduced order, prosperity, intelligence, and piety, among a people as destitute, when he went to them, as the most savage tribes could possibly be. The whole of a long life he dedicated to this great work. The infant school system of instruction, now so general, owes its origin to Oberlin ; and the piety and apostolic simplicity of his character made him a model of excellence to all thoughtful minds.

It is interesting to trace the home influences that contributed to develop so much worth, and his biographers remark, that "To his pious and accomplished mother he often acknowledged himself indebted for his love of the things 'that are excellent,' and for the desires he subsequently felt of dedicating his talents and his powers for the good of others.   She was indeed a truly admirable woman, and conscientiously endeavored to bring up her children in 'the nurture and adminition of the Lord.' She was in the habit of assembling them together every evening, and of reading aloud some instructive book, whilst they sat around the table copying pictures, which their father had drawn for them; and scarcely a night passed, but, when on the point of separating, there was a general request, for 'one beautiful hymn from dear mamma,' with which she always complied. The hymn was followed by a prayer; and thus their infant steps were conducted to Him who has said, 'Suffer little children to come unto me.'"

It was through the instrumentality of this admirable mother, that during Oberlin's youth, he was savingly converted to God. A celebrated preacher, named Dr. Lorentz, excited a great sensation in Strasbourg, by the ardent zeal with which he preached a crucified Saviour. Oberlin's mother, attracted by the general report, went to hear him, and was so much struck with the powerful manner in which he set forth the grand doctrines of redemption and remisson of sin, that she entreated her favorite son (John Frederic) to accompany her on the following Sunday. Being a student in the theological class at the University, and having been warned by his superiors not to go, it was with some reluctance that he suffered his mother to persuade him to accompany her. In compliance with her urgent solicitations, he, however, at last acceded, and was so much delighted with the evangelical truths he heard preached, that he became a regular and diligent attendant of the doctor's sermons, and this circumstance probably contributed to strengthen his religious impressions, and to confirm him in the resolution he had made in childhood.

The mother of Oberlin had the unspeakable satisfaction of beholding her son solemnly dedicate himself to the service of God at the age of twenty ; a reward the greatest that maternal piety could receive.

------------

## MRS. ANNE THORNTON'S ADDRESS TO HER CHILDREN, &c., DURING HER LAST SICKNESS.

KNOWING whom she had believed, and expecting to be soon with Him to behold his glory, she employed the remnant of her breath in praising him, in praying for others, in instructing, admonishing, and comforting her children and friends who were with her. " My children," said she, " I dearly love, but I am willing to leave them. I hope they will follow me to heaven. I have endeavored to recommend the best things, and can only lament that I have not set them a better example. But, if any infirmity or sin they have seen in me have proved a hinderance to them, I pray God to take the remembrance of it from their minds, and enable them to look to that perfect pattern, who has left us an example how we ought to walk." To her daughter she said,—" Study the Scriptures, not only as containing truths which are able to make you wise

unto salvation, which they do in the fullest manner ;
but read them for rules of life, for history, for description of characters, for geography, for everything. One
thing which gives history its excellence, is its authenticity : another is the character of its author.   Now,
the Bible is infallibly true ; the Bible is the book of
God.   It not only instructs us in the knowledge of
God, of ourselves, and of the way by which we may
approach him with hope ; but in whatever is needful
for us to know ; and it will both please and profit
every person, who reads it with attention and prayer."
A little while after, she charged her daughter, Maria,
to tell her other children, "that living or dying, their
mother loved them.   You have been good and pleasant
children to me, and I pray you, take the Apostle's
advice—' Be ye kindly affectioned, one toward another ;
be ye holy, harmless, undefiled.'   My dear Maria, you
have nursed me affectionately, and now you are called
to an affecting scene,—a dying mother parting with a
child she dearly loves.   After I am gone, and you
retire in secret to weep, perhaps your mother may be
looking on : I charge you and your dear sisters, let not
a thought enter your minds, that you have neglected
anything that could have been done for me.   You have
all been kind : I have had every attention shown me
that could have been given ; the Lord bless you all.
Do not expect too much from each other, and then you
will live in love."   After a short silence, she said—
"The mystery of the cross contains our all of good—our
Redeemer, our great deliverer, is our surety and our

peace. I have no hope, no plea, but Lord, thou hast died. Oh! Maria, he must be your salvation; expect only to be saved through him." Next day, her other two daughters arrived. She said—" My sweet Anne (I cannot say my dearest child, for you are all equally dear to me)—my precious Harriet, seek the God of your fathers: he is my support and my all; my faithful God." Seeing them weep, she observed, " I love your tears; they are precious, because they are tears of affection; but you may weep too much. Take care that you do not indulge excessive grief." After discoursing some time on redemption, she added—" O, may the Holy Spirit impress these truths upon your hearts, my dear children! Without his influence, all is nothing. My mother," she continued, "was a blessed woman, and I sometimes think she will be one of the first happy spirits to welcome me home. How I shall rejoice in a future day to present my children to her in glory! My dear children, let no one cheat you out of immortality." It was told her that one of her nieces was committing to memory Gambold's " Mystery of Life," on which she gave a smile of approbation; and turning to her children, entreated them to fill their minds with the good things which might be useful to them on a dying bed. Then, looking affectionately upon them, she said—" My dear children, you see your dying parent bearing testimony to the truths of God."

She expired without a struggle, March 12th, 1799.

## MRS. ELIZA BERRY AND HER CHILDREN.

MRS. ELIZA BERRY, the wife of the Rev. Jos. Berry, some time pastor of the Dissenting church at Warminster, was the youngest daughter of Rev. Thomas Grove, formerly of Woodburn, in the county of Bucks, who was one of the six students expelled from the University of Oxford, for praying, reading, and expounding the Scriptures.

Descended from a family of great respectability, she had been favored with a good education, and was not destitute of those elegant accomplishments which would have fitted her to shine in polite society. The event which was chiefly instrumental in her conversion was the pious conversation of an amiable brother-in-law, who, at the same time, and by the same means, succeeded in producing a permanent impression upon the mind of her sister. She was married to Mr. Berry in the year 1804; and after a lingering illness, expired February 18th, 1812, in the 37th year of her age.

Such are the few particulars which we have been able to gather of her history. But her character was of no ordinary stamp; and it is for the sake of laying this before our readers, that we have introduced the present brief memoir. We are indebted for the following interesting portrait of the Christian wife and mother to the pen of the Rev. Wm. Jay, of Bath, who preached a sermon on the occasion of her death, which has been printed.

" The religion of this saint," says Mr. Jay, " was not *occasional;* it did not depend upon particular seasons, and exercises, and occurrences. She was in the fear of the Lord all the day long, and acknowledged Him in all her ways. No one loved the habitation of God's house more than she did, but her devotion was not confined to it. It was not roving and hearing religion. It appeared in public, but it lived in private. It was closet and family religion. It was not a thing separable from her, and which was sometimes assumed, and sometimes laid aside; but it was a principle wrought into all her feelings, habits, and actions. Let me adduce a partial but interesting illustration.

" After the month of November, 1811, she scarcely ever went out. Her Sabbath-day evenings were employed in reading the Scriptures, and holding familiar dialogues with her three babes. After hearing them repeat a short prayer, and one of Watts' little hymns for children, she seated them each in a separate chair, while, with maternal simplicity and endearment, she heard and answered *their* questions and proposed her *own*. Dismissing the younger two to rest, the eldest, then six years old, was retained up a little longer. With him, her constant Sabbath-day evening custom was to pray. At these periods she forgot herself in endeavoring to interest her boy. She would begin to pray for his father, who, at that precise period, was preaching. Then she would pray for her children, one by one. After mentioning their names, she either implored forgiveness for foibles, or expressed her gratitude that the 'great God had made them such good children.' Taking this boy one day into the parlor where she usually performed these exercises, his father asked him, 'if his dear mother did not sometimes kneel with him and pray?' With eyes instantly filled with tears, the little disciple artlessly replied, 'Yes, father, mother used to kneel at that chair, and hold my hand, and pray for father that he may do good, and for me, and for Henry, and for little Mary, and for all of us.'

"O, ye mothers, sanctify your tenderness, and your influence! How much depends upon your gentle and early endeavors! How often you may sow the seed, which, after a lapse of time, shall revive and flourish, thirty, sixty, and a hundred-fold! How often has a disobedient son been reclaimed by the remembrance of the eloquent tears of her who bore him, or the pressure of her trembling hand, when delivering her dying charge! What did Mr. Cecil and Mr. Newton owe to the lessons their mothers had taught them? What did Timothy owe to his grandmother, Lois, and his mother, Eunice? What did Samuel owe to Hannah? We know little of Jesse; but how often and tenderly does David, in his devotions, refer to his mother, and plead the relation in which he had the honor and happiness of standing to her—'Save the son of *thine handmaid*.' 'Truly I am thy servant, and son of *thine handmaid*.'

"'I think,' said this deceased mother, about a fortnight before her death, 'I think, in looking back on all these seasons, my sweetest exercises were with my dear boy on the Sabbath evenings. The house was still; my babes were in bed; my husband was laboring for God in the sanctuary; everything aided and inspired devotion. I think my dear boy will never forget some of these seasons any more than myself. O, my happy seasons with my infant son!'

"Her attention to order and regularity was singular. Life was with her a system, and everything in it had its due time and importance. Hence she knew nothing of that hurry and fretfulness occasioned by omission and confusion. She, in her last illness, looked forward, and arranged everything, however minute. On giving up her books as secretary, a few weeks before she died, her countenance was a true index of her mind. When the ladies were gone, she exclaimed—' Blessed be God for this. I should not have liked my husband or my children to have been reproached with inaccurate accounts. Above all, I should have been sorry for the cause of religion to suffer.'

"During her illness, she had frequently requested Christian friends to pray that she might have an easy dismissal. Her wish was granted. She seemed free from pain. Her last broken, and almost inarticulate accents were, 'Valley — shadow — home — Jesus — peace.' A few minutes before eight, her head gently dropped on one side of her pillow, and her last pulse was felt by the hand of her anguished husband.

"The deceased was only a private character, it is true; but she was a decided character: she was a constant character: she was an amiable character: she was an inoffensive character: she was a benevolent character.

She neither lived nor died to herself.   And, 'he that
in these things serveth Christ, is acceptable to God,
and approved of men.'"

---

## GENERAL WASHINGTON AND HIS MOTHER.

GEORGE WASHINGTON was born in Westmoreland
County, Virginia, on the 22d February, 1732.  He was
the eldest son, by a second marriage, of Augustine
Washington, a gentleman of large property, the de-
scendant of John Washington, an Englishman, who
had emigrated to America during the government of
Oliver Cromwell.   The name of Washington's mother
was Mary Ball.   Her husband dying suddenly in the
year 1743, the charge of educating a large family, consisting of two surviving sons of her husband by his
former wife, and five surviving children of her own, devolved upon her.   George Washington was not quite
eleven years of age at the time of his father's death.

Although cut off in the prime of life, Augustine
Washington left all his children well provided for.
Lawrence, the eldest, was left an estate of twenty-five
hundred acres, besides shares in iron works in Maryland
and Virginia ; Augustine, who was next oldest, inherited
an estate in Westmoreland ; George inherited the house
and lands in Stafford County, where his father resided
at the time of his death ; his three younger brothers had
each a plantation of six or seven hundred acres assigned him ; and provision was otherwise made for the sis-

10*

ter. By the will of her husband, Mrs. Washington
was entrusted with the sole management of the property of her five children, until they should respectively
come of age. Being a woman of singular prudence
and strength of character, she fulfilled this important
charge with great success. She lived to see her eldest
son at the height of his greatness.

His biographers have said—"To the care of his excellent and *pious* mother, he was indebted for that education and those sentiments of heroism, and principles
of virtue and honor, which, acting on a happy disposition and a lofty genius, and aided by a favorable con-
currence of circumstances, raised him to the summit
of greatness and glory. Washington continued at
school until his fifteenth year, when a sort of crisis
took place in his history, which brings his mother's
character very affectingly before us.

"His elder brother, Lawrence, observing a military
turn in George, obtained a commission for him as a
midshipman in the British navy, thinking by this means
to advance his interests. It appears that the youth
himself was pleased with the prospect, and prepared
with alacrity to enter into that profession. The consent of his fond and faithful mother had to be obtained ; and she, yielding to her deep tenderness, could
not consent to her son entering upon so dangerous a
pursuit. In fact, she could not part with him. Relations blamed her as 'a fond, unthinking mother,' but
it was owing to these yearnings of her maternal love,
that, under Divine Providence, the whole career of her

son was indebted.  Had he entered the British navy, it is probable his name would never have been heard of; and his country's destinies might have been very different.

"The ardent youth yielded obedience to his mother's wishes, and resigned the plan which in his heart he concurred in, and Providence opened another and a brighter path for him.

"The character of a warrior is not one we would present for admiration; but Washington was as great in peace as he was victorious in conquest; and compared with all warriors of ancient and modern times, he is, beyond all others, humane, just, magnanimous, and patriotic.  The emancipator of his country, his name is never pronounced without reverence, and when his warlike work was done, he retired into private life, and became as much beloved for the gentler virtues, as he had been admired for the greatness of his genius, and the splendor of his achievements."

---

## REV. JOHN BELFRAGE, OF FALKIRK, AND HIS MOTHER.

He was born at Colleston, County of Kinross, Scotland, Feb. 2d, 1736.  His father was distinguished by his good sense and patriotic spirit; being particularly active in promoting improvements, conciliating differences, and managing the interests of the young, committed by dying parents to his care.  His mother was the only child of the Rev. Andrew Ure, minister of Tossaway. In her, *good sense, enlargement of mind, and fervent piety, were associated with all the gentler dispositions. The tuition of such a mother must be the greatest value* to the young. The tenderness of her heart gives her peculiar powers of persuasion, and religion never appears so lovely to a child as when its ardor glows on a mother's countenance, nor its lessons so melting as when they are enforced by her tears, and followed by her prayers. She marked with pleasure her son's early inclination for the ministry. To prepare him for this sacred office, she labored to form pious sentiments in his mind, and to cherish devout feelings in his heart; and the symptoms of a gracious character, which she discovered in the rising youth, gave her the greatest delight. This desire for the ministry was strengthened by the visits which he paid to his grandfather. Young as he was, he marked with deep interest the piety of his manner, the calmness of his dwelling, his studious habits, his delight in the service of God, and his beneficent care of his parish. Nor did he ever forget the solemnity and kindness of the venerable man, when, like Jacob blessing his grandsons, he laid his hand on his head and besought the God who had fed him all his life long to bless the child. At a suitable age John went to the College of Edinburgh; and while there, through preserving grace, and the Divine blessing on a religious education, his conduct was exemplary. Some time after this, he was deprived by death of his invaluable mother. The parting, after a visit which he paid her in her illness, was solemn and affecting to them both.    She felt that she should see his face no more; and while he stood weeping by her couch, she expressed her firm hope in Christ: soothed him by various assurances of Divine guidance and consolation, exhorted him to a close walk with God, and with a voice which sunk into his heart, gave him a Christian mother's last blessing.    September 6th, 1758, he was ordained to the pastoral care of a congregation at Falkirk, and in this situation he continued till his death.    Here, for forty years, *he was a burning and a shining light.*    His private life, his domestic conduct, and his public ministry, were all directed by the same holy principles.    He was frequently deputed to restore societies at variance to harmony; and for this labor of love, he was singularly qualified by his meekness and prudence.    By his influence, dissensions in families, in neighborhoods, and in congregations, have been healed; and he has left the place which has been the dark scene of animosity and strife, with blessings on his head from those whose happiness has been restored by the return of concord and benevolence.    His mild and affectionate disposition prepared him for the enjoyment of social comforts.    Two years after his ordination, he was married to a young lady in his own congregation, whom God made an eminent blessing to him and to their family.    His home was the rest of his heart.    His solicitude for the welfare of his partner and children was tender and constant.    The seasons which he set apart for private devotion were marked by the youngest with reverential interest; and from the closet of prayer he returned with a countenance the index of a heart sanctified and gladdened by piety, to bless his household by the intercourse of kindness, and the counsels of wisdom. It was his delight to say or do whatever would contribute to its happiness. His attention to the religious instruction of his family was not confined to the evenings of the Lord's day, but was often manifested at other seasons. There was such a sweetness in his mode of teaching, that the scene and hour of tuition was never gloomy, but always pleasant. He listened to the tasks of his children not merely with patience, but with evident interest. His advices were singularly solemn, tender, and appropriate; and the directions he gave them as to prayer were happily adapted to guide the youthful mind to devotion. It was his care to obtain for them suitable books, and to examine what information they had derived, and what impressions they had felt in the perusal; and such were often his inquiries after their attendance on religious ordinances. These interesting duties were seconded with unwearied assiduity, by the pious and enlightened care of a mother, whose heart was devoted to their best interests. When two of his sons, at the most promising season of life, were taken from him by death,—like a truly Christian parent, he labored to assuage the grief of his family, and thus expressed his devout acquiescence in the will of heaven: "I must say with Jacob, 'Joseph is not, and Simeon is not,' but with him I will not say, 'all these

things are against me ;' for that is no longer mine which
God claims, and I believe that his darkest paths are
mercy."   His fourth son was educated for the ministry ; and never, (to use his own words) " never can be
forgot the solemn representations of his father, of the
piety, wisdom, and zeal required in that office, of its
tremendous responsibility, of the rewards promised to
the faithful pastor, and of the doom of him who should
disgrace that function by the spirit of the world, or
the error of the wicked.   He felt the deepest interest
in the progress of his studies ; and when he was licensed to preach the Gospel, this was the animating charge
by which he encouraged one so young, under a trust
so solemn, " *My son, be strong in the grace that is in
Christ Jesus.*"   When this promising young man was
appointed to be his colleague and successor, Mr. Bel-
frage regarded it as the sanction of heaven to a relation which should unite his son more closely to him.
He rejoiced in it, not merely as what might be his
solace in advanced life, and a comfort to his family, but
as likely to maintain the peace of his congregation ;
and most earnest were his prayers that it might contribute to advance their best interests.   When the ordination took place, his exhortations on that occasion
were solemn, affectionate, and faithful, like those of
David to Solomon, his son, when he said to him—
" Thou Solomon, my son, know thou the God of thy
Father, and serve him with a perfect heart and a willing mind ; for the Lord searcheth all hearts, and un-
derstandeth all the imaginations of the thoughts ; if

thou seek him he will be found of thee; but if thou forsake him he will cast thee off forever."—1 Chronicles xxviii. 9. The youngest in the families of his charge said they loved him, he was so mild and so good. He was delighted to see them happy, and by tracing their tempers and capacity, he would suggest his pious counsels, in language so simple as to be understood, and in the most engaging manner. Having attained a good old age, amidst the esteem and love both of his congregation and family, he was taken ill, and obliged to abandon his sacred work. The venerable sufferer cheered and comforted his sorrowing household. To his wife he said, "Thy Maker is thine husband." To his children—"I have left you all in God." On the last Sabbath of his life, when his son and some other of his family came in from public worship, he said,—"My heart was with you; I am trying to raise it to the temple above, where a rest, a Sabbath remaineth for the people of God. I have long preached salvation by Christ, my wish is to join the great multitude above." And with his eyes turned to his family, he added, "and to be joined by all I love on earth, in singing salvation to God, and to the Lamb forever." He spoke frequently, in his illness, of his congregation; expressed his satisfaction that they were not deprived of any religious ordinance by his affliction; commended them to the care of the Shepherd and Bishop of souls; implored his gracious acceptance of his ministry, and earnestly prayed that the kingdom of Christ might flourish among them. To his son, he said, " I have been committing you to the care of the Great Apostle and High Priest of our profession. He will be the guide of your youth, and in the light and grace of His presence, you shall not miss a father's counsels or kindness." When he felt his end approaching, he expressed, in a faltering voice, his attachment to his family, declaring that Christ was all his hope, and his parting intercession and blessing was his last expression of piety and love. In a short time after he entered into rest, and like David, *having served his generation according to the will of God, he fell asleep.*

---

## THE REV. RICHARD CECIL AND HIS MOTHER.

Mr. Cecil was born in Chiswell Street, London, Nov. 8th, 1748. His father and grandfather were scarlet dyers to the East India Company. His mother was the only child of Mr. Grosvenor, a merchant, in London, and brother to the Rev. Dr. Grosvenor, the well-known author of the "Mourner." To many other excellent traits in her character, may be added, her benevolence to the poor. In order to enlarge her resources, she employed herself in working fine work, according to the fashion of the day, which she sold for their benefit. Richard was born after his mother was fifty years old; during her travail with this son of her old age, her heart was overwhelmed with sorsow. Yet this child was the comfort and honor of her latter days! In his childhood, Mr. Cecil was

11

often exposed to imminent danger, and only preserved by evident divine interposition. The following is a remarkable instance. His father had in the ground, near his dye-house, several large backs of water, one of which was sunk into the earth, and in winter was frequently covered with ice. A hole was made in the ice for the purpose of supplying the horses with water. At this hole Richard was playing with a stick, till he suddenly plunged under the ice. The men had received particular orders over night, to go to work in a part of the dye-house from which this piece of water was not visible; but for reasons which could not be assigned, they went to work at an opposite part, where it was directly before their eyes. One of the men thought he saw a scarlet cloak appear at the hole broke in the ice, and resolved to go and see what it was; in attempting to take it out, he discovered it to be the scarlet coat of his young master. He was taken out apparently dead; but, after long effort, was recovered. This child of Providence had early religious impressions. These were first received from Janeway's "Token for Children," which his mother gave him when he was about six years of age. "I was much affected by this book," said he, "and recollect that I wept, and got into a corner, where I prayed that I also might have 'an interest in Christ,' like one of the children there mentioned, though I did not then know what the expression meant." Those impressions, however, wore away. He fell into the follies and vices of youth, and, by degrees, began to listen to infidel principles, till he avowed himself openly

an unbeliever. Even at this period, and indeed throughout his whole life, he acted on principles of honor and
integrity.   One instance is both singular and pleasing.
When he was but a little boy, his father went on business to the India House, and took Richard with him.
While he was transacting his business, his son was dismissed, and directed to wait for him at one of the doors.
His father, on finishing his business, went out at another door, and entirely forgot that he had ordered his
son to wait for him.   In the evening, his mother, missing the child, inquired where he was; on which his
father, recollecting his directions, said, "You may
depend on it, he is still waiting where I appointed
him."   He immediately returned to the India House,
and found him on the spot where he had been ordered
to wait.   He knew that his father expected him to wait,
and would not disappoint him.   Though he had cast
off the yoke of religion, *yet the effect of parental influence, and of early education, was still powerful and salutary.*   He himself said afterward to his parents, " *The
spirit and tone of your house will have great influence
on your children.   If it is what it ought to be, it will*
often fasten conviction on their minds, however wicked
they may become; I have felt the truth of this in my
own case; I said, ' My father is right, and I am wrong;
Oh, *let me die the death of the righteous, and let my last
end be like his!'*   The bye conversations of a family
are, in this view, of unspeakable importance.   On the
whole, arguments addressed to the heart press more
forcibly than those addressed to the head.   When I

was a child, and a very wicked one, too, one of Dr.
Watts's hymns sent me to weep in a corner. I felt
the influence of faith in suffering Christians. The
character of young Samuel came home to me, when
nothing else had any hold on my mind." And again,
" Where parental influence does not convert, it hampers.
It hangs on the wheels of evil. *I had a pious mother,
who dropped things in my way; I could never rid myself of them.* I liked to be an infidel in company,
rather than when alone. I was wretched when by
myself. I could not divest myself of my better principles. I went with one of my companions to see 'the
Minor.' The ridicule on regeneration was high sport
to him: to me it was none; it could not move my features. He knew no difference between regeneration
and transubstantiation. I did: I knew there was such
a thing. I was afraid and ashamed to laugh at it. Parental influence thus cleaves to a man; it harasses him;
it throws itself continually in his way. My mother
would talk to me, and weep as she talked. I flung out
of the house with an oath, but wept, too, when I got
into the street. My father had a religious servant. I
frequently cursed and reviled him. He would only
smile on me. That went to my heart; I felt that he
looked on me as a deluded creature; I felt that he
thought he had something which I knew not how to
value, and that he was therefore greatly my superior;
I felt there was real dignity in his conduct. It made
me appear little even in my own eyes." For this daring offender, however, God had mercy in reserve. *He*

*was the child of many tears, instructions, admonitions, and prayers;* and though now a prodigal, grace soon restored and saved him. Lying one night in bed, he was contemplating the case of his mother. "I see," said he within himself, "two unquestionable facts : first, my mother is greatly afflicted—in circumstances, body, and mind—and yet I see that she cheerfully bears up under all, by the support she derives from constantly retiring to her closet and her Bible : secondly, that she has a secret spring of comfort of which I know nothing; while I, who give an unbounded loose to my appetites, and seek pleasure by every means, seldom or never find it. If, however, there is any such secret in religion, why may I not attain it as well as my mother ? I will immediately seek it of GOD." He instantly rose in his bed and began to pray. But he was soon damped in his attempt, by recollecting that much of his mother's comfort seemed to arise from her faith in Christ. "Now," thought he, "this Christ I have ridiculed; he stands much in my way, and can form no part of my prayers." In utter confusion of mind, therefore, he lay down again. Next day, he continued to pray to "the Supreme Being;" he began to consult books, and to attend preachers; his difficulties were gradually removed, and his objections answered; and his course of life began to amend. He now listened to the pious admonitions of his mother, which he had before affected to receive with pride and scorn; yet they had fixed themselves in his heart like a barbed arrow. Now, he would discourse with her, and hear her, without out-

11*

rage, which led her to hope that a gracious principle was forming in his heart. Light broke into his mind, till he found that Jesus Christ was *the* only *way, the truth, and the life, to all that come unto God through him.* At the desire of his father, he now went to Queen's College, Oxford, in 1773. He was ordained in 1776, and entered on his ministry with zeal, faithfulness, and success. In June, 1777, he lost his pious mother, whose death was made of a singular benefit to him. His father also died in Feb., 1779. As a husband, a father, a master, Mr. Cecil was most exemplary. His mourning widow says—"In our family worship, the Scripture was read by one of the children. While the passage was reading, he frequently interspersed short, pithy, and instructive remarks, in the most easy and familiar manner. Of his prayers, I can only say, that I never did, nor do I ever expect, to hear any like them, in simplicity, unction and devotion, and in the filial fear, affection, and reverence, which bespoke much nearness and close friendship with his God and Saviour."

"Christian parents," says the Rev. Josiah Pratt, "and especially Christian mothers, may gather from the history and character of our departed friend, every possible encouragement to the unwearied care of their children." While St. Augustine, and Bishop Hall, R. Hooker, John Newton, R. Cecil, and many other great and eminent servants of Christ, have left on record their grateful acknowledgments to their pious mothers, as the instruments, under God, of winning them to him-

self, let no woman despair respecting even her most
untoward child.

----

## REV. JAMES KIDD, D.D., AND HIS MOTHER.

Late Minister of Gilcomston Church, and Professor of Oriental
Languages in Marischal College, Aberdeen.

JAMES KIDD was born of humble, yet respectable
parents, near Loughbrickland, in the county of Down,
Ireland, on the 6th November, 1761.  Soon after his
birth, he had the misfortune to lose his father, and his
mother then removed to Broughshane, in the county
of Antrim, where James received the first rudiments
of his education.  From the first leaf of the Shorter
Catechism, he was taught the alphabet *by his mother,*
and after spelling and reading each question in rota-
tion, he committed the whole to memory.  Thus was
he grounded, in the early years of childhood, in the
doctrines of that church of which he became so distinguished a member.  His memory, too, was cultivated by exercise at a period when that faculty is rarely
called into action; and to this circumstance may be
mainly attributed those wonderfully retentive powers
which supplied, at will, to his capacious mind the rich
stores of ancient and modern literature.

Having mastered his theological horn-book, his mother provided him with a copy of the New Testament,
and carefully superintended his perusal of this sacred
volume.  Commencing with the Gospel of St. John,

the pious matron caused him daily to commit to memory the passage he had just read; but what he experienced most useful in after-life from her instructions, was the particular manner in which she pointed out Jesus Christ in every place where his name was mentioned, uniformly inquiring of her pupil, "Who Christ was? What he did? What he said?" showing how mysterious he was as God and man, and how graciously and powerfully he exhibited himself in all his parables and miracles. This was real instruction; and it laid a foundation on which her pupil raised an immortal superstructure.

Under such instructions, his mind caught a flame of love for the New Testament. He reposed with it under his pillow at night. It was his last care when going to sleep, and his first when he awoke. His mind expanded in the knowledge of the Scriptures, and his memory became retentive of their truths. When about eight years of age, he went to the Presbyterian Meeting House of Broughshane (of which his mother was a member), on a Communion Sabbath. Agreeably to the ancient usage of the Scottish Kirk, it was at that time customary for Presbyterian clergymen to be habited in blue when dispensing the Lord's Supper. The appearance of the minister (the Rev. Charles Brown) in this singular dress, the snow-white covering of the sacramental table, the view of the holy elements, the solemnity of the subjects, and the devotion of the people, made an indelible impression on his young mind; and he frequently declared that on that day, and in

that place, he formed the resolution of using every
endeavor to become qualified for being a preacher of
the Gospel of Christ. To the attainment of his wishes,
however, there were many obstacles—the most serious
of which was pecuniary disability. Determined to
make the attempt, he borrowed a copy of Wittenhall's
Latin Grammar, and began repeating lessons to a
young man, named James Ritchie, who was accounted
the best Latin scholar then attending the school, taught
by Mr. Linton, in the neighborhood, and who became
exceedingly attached to young Kidd, and assiduously
labored to promote his improvement. It was now that
the embryo professor of languages set to work in earnest. The intensity of his application so absorbed every
thought, that his mind was both night and day upon
the stretch. He awoke frequently in the silence of
night, and lighting what in the country is called a *split*,
looked at any passage in which he found himself de-
ficient, and having mastered the difficulty, consigned
himself again to sleep. At the age of nine, he accustomed himself to rise by the first glimpse of dawn, and
from that time till his last illness, he continued to inculcate and practice early rising. In this manner he
pursued his Latin studies through the Grammar Vo-
cabulary, Corderius, and Justin, when death deprived
him of his friend and benefactor, Ritchie. New difficulties now presented themselves; but so much had
his industry and perseverance attracted general notice,
that Mr. Allan, a neighboring farmer, placed him for
six months at the school which Ritchie had attended.

Here he made rapid progress in the study of Latin, while writing and arithmetic were not neglected; and when he left school, scarcely ten years of age, he was able, with the assistance of such class-books as he could procure on loan, to become his own instructor.

Britain having acknowledged the independence of her late colonies in America, Mr. Kidd formed the resolution of emigrating to that country, in the hope of being able to push his fortune. He accordingly embarked for Philadelphia, with Mrs. Kidd, in April, 1784. He carried with him no letters of introduction, and, consequently, on his arrival, he had no friends to welcome him. On the recommendation of Mr. Little, a schoolmaster in the neighborhood, he undertook the tuition of a family, near New Jersey, and soon after became preceptor in a family in Maryland. After this he removed to Philadelphia, and took part with Mr. Little in the labor of conducting his school. And soon afterward, he was induced to open a classical academy —an undertaking which proved very successful. A vacancy for an usher having occurred in the College of Pennsylvania, Mr. Kidd became a candidate, and was elected to the situation. While acting in this capacity, he was enrolled a student in the University, where he went through a regular academical course. During this time, he was also employed as a corrector for the press, and in this situation he first saw the Hebrew alphabet. In a very short time he became perfectly master of the letters and points, and placed himself under the tuition of a Portuguese Jew, by whose instructions, and his own intense application, he became familiar with the Book of Genesis in the course of a few months.

At this period, Mr. Kidd's finances were reduced to a very low ebb, owing to the exorbitant charges of his Jewish teacher, and the expenses consequent on a rising family. With extreme parsimony, he had accumulated as many dollars as would purchase a suit of clothes, of which he stood very much in want; but he had likewise, for some time, cast his eyes wistfully upon a Hebrew Bible, in the shop of a Dutch bookseller, to obtain which was to him an object of extreme solicitude. He had repeatedly called on purpose to see the much-wished-for treasure; and oftentimes, in passing, he looked at it through the window. While going in quest of the new suit, he went near the bookshop. The Bible caught his eye, and that glance was sufficient. The cash was in hand, and his heart greedy for the long-coveted object,—the Dutchman was loud in his encomiums on the excellence of the type and the edition. It was enough; our young Hebraist threw down the money, destined for another purpose, and carrying off his prize in triumph, began again, with humility and resignation, to accumulate, by private teaching and correcting the press, the sum requisite to replace his threadbare garments by new ones. He now occasionally attended a Jewish Synagogue, where he learned to read Hebrew fluently, and became intimately acquainted with the peculiarities of the language and the Jewish ceremonies. Oriental languages became his favorite study; and two designs occupied his thoughts, namely, traveling in the East, or studying divinity in Scotland.   He was induced to abandon the former by his intimate friend, the celebrated Dr. Benjamin Rush, of Philadelphia.   At length he embarked for Scotland, carrying with him letters of introduction to many of the most eminent literary characters in Edinburgh.   By their advice, he, a second time, commenced a course of academical study, and was enrolled a student of divinity of the Established Church of Scotland.   While attending the various duties at College he opened classes under the immediate patronage of the celebrated Rabbi Robertson, as a teacher of Oriental languages; and his success in this undertaking was so eminent, that when the professorship of Oriental languages in the Marischal College of Aberdeen became vacant by the death of Dr. Donaldson, he was, on the recommendation of Drs. Hill and Erskine, and other distinguished individuals, appointed to fill that chair.   In 1793, Mr. Kidd went to Aberdeen and began the duties of his office, which he performed with honor to himself, and advantage to the numerous ministers of the Gospel of Christ, who studied the original of the Sacred Scriptures under his care.   By his instrumentality the knowledge and study of Hebrew was revived in the north of Scotland, where this language had been comparatively dormant for a great many years.

Although he had studied divinity for two sessions in the University of Edinburgh, he was so anxious to perfect himself for the ministry, that he attended four successive courses at the theological halls of King's and Marischal Colleges; after which he was licensed as a preacher of the Gospel by the Presbytery of Aberdeen.

Shortly afterward he was appointed evening lecturer in the Trinity Chapel, Aberdeen, where he continued to officiate for five years. On the 18th June, 1807, he was ordained minister of the Chapel of Ease, Gilcomston, in the immediate neighborhood of Aberdeen, where he dispensed the bread of life to perhaps the most numerous congregation in Scotland, until the period of his death, which took place on the 24th of December, 1834, in the seventy-third year of his age.

In 1818 the College of New Jersey conferred on Professor Kidd the unsolicited degree of Doctor in Divinity; an honor to which his superior talents gave him an unquestionable claim.

Deeply impressed with the responsibility attached to his character as a minister of the everlasting Gospel, Dr. Kidd labored in the discharge of his duty with an assiduity that has seldom been equaled. The dying and the afflicted, the widow and the orphan, were the objects of his daily care; and while he strenuously exerted himself for the relief of their temporal wants, he poured the consolations of religion into their wounded spirits, and taught them to lay their burdens upon Him who alone can adminster comfort to the dying and balm to the afflicted, and who is the husband of the widow, and the orphan's stay.

12

### DR. BUCHANAN AND HIS MOTHER.

#### BY THE REV. HUGH PEARSON.

CLAUDIUS BUCHANAN was born at Cambuslang, near Glasgow, March 12th, 1766. His mother was the daughter of Mr. Claudius Somers, an elder of the Church of Scotland. Both these excellent persons trained up the youthful object of their care, from his earliest years, in religious principles and habits. He himself often recollected, in future life, the serious impressions that were made upon his mind at this period, by the devotion observed in his father's house, and by the admonitions which his affectionate and pious grandfather was accustomed to address to him occasionally in his study. And though, as it will afterward appear, the instructions and example of his pious relatives were not immediately productive of any decided and permanent effect, yet he must be added to the number of those who ultimately derived essential benefit from having been brought up "*in the nurture and admonition of the Lord,*" and as affording *fresh encouragement to religious parents to pursue a course which has been so frequently crowned with happy success.* Young Buchanan was sent to school at the age of seven, where he remained for several years. About his fourteenth or fifteenth year, his religious impressions revived, which he communicated to his excellent grandfather, who carefully cherished them, and assured him of his prayers. For a few months he continued in this promising course, spending much time in devotion amongst the rocks on the sea-shore; but at length his serious thoughts were dissi-pated by the society of an irreligious companion, and his goodness, like that of many a hopeful youth, van-isshed "as a morning cloud, and as the early dew;" nor was it till many years afterward, that painful and salutary convictions led him to seek that God whose early invitations he had ungratefully refused. From his childhood, Claudius was intended by his parents for the ministry; but as he grew up to manhood, he so far lost his sense of piety to God, and duty to his pa-rents, as to set out with the romantic design of making the tour of Europe on foot; and in order to prevent any opposition to his scheme from his relatives, he pre-tended that he had been invited by an English gentle-man to accompany his son upon a journey to the Con-tinent; and he displayed the advantages of this en-gagement in so flattering a light to his father and mother, as to procure their consent. Thus were they deceived by their own child. A rash undertaking like this, commenced in guilt and folly, could not be ex-pected to succeed. Young Buchanan was destitute of pecuniary resources, and therefore proposed to support himself through his projected journey as an itinerant musician. He was, however, heartily tired of his men-dicant life before he reached the borders of England, and would gladly have returned home; but pride would not suffer him to confess his faults to his parents, and ask their forgiveness. He therefore embarked in a vessel at North Shields, and sailed for London. A storm arose during the voyage, and the perverse young man felt that the judgment of God, as in the case of Jonah, was now overtaking him. His merciful Father watched over him in the hour of danger, and spared him for future usefulness. On the 2d of September, he arrived safely in London. " But by this time," he himself observed, "my spirits were nearly exhausted by distress and poverty. I now relinquished every idea of going abroad." He did not yet feel his sin in a proper manner. But supporting himself in London by writing, and often experiencing hardships and privations, he still corresponded with his friends in Scotland, *as from abroad*, dating his fictitious letters from various parts of the Continent, and always giving them flattering accounts of his health and situation. In about a year after his departure, his father died, Aug. 24th, 1788. Notwithstanding this solemn event, he still continued to deceive his widowed and affectionate mother. During this period, he was restless and unhappy. His conscience warned and reproached him. *The religious principles imbibed in youth operated as a salutary restraint, and preserved him from some temptations.* At times, he would seriously reflect on his improper conduct, attend upon divine worship, bow his knee in prayer, and resolve upon a new life. At length, in 1790, after three years had been spent in wandering from the way of peace, it pleased God to bring the prodigal to himself. " In the month of June last," he writes, in Feb. 1791, "on a Sunday evening, a serious young man called upon me. Among other things, I asked him, whether he believed there was such a thing as divine grace. He took occasion from this inquiry to enlarge much on the subject; spoke with zeal and earnestness, and chiefly in Scripture language; and concluded with a very affecting address to the conscience and the heart. While he spoke I listened to him with earnestness, and before I was aware, a most powerful impression was made upon my mind. I reflected on my past sins with horror, and spent the night I know not how. The next day my fears wore off a little, but they soon returned. I anxiously waited the arrival of Sunday, but when it came, I found no relief. After some time, I communicated my situation to my religious friend; he prayed with me ; and next Sunday I went with him to hear an eminent minister." He now prayed often, read pious books—Doddridge's Rise and Progress of Religion in the Soul, Alleine's Alarm to the Unconverted, and Boston's Fourfold State—and sought with deep concern the salvation of his soul. He concludes this narrative with a most emphatic sentence : " Nothing but the hand of the Almighty who created me can change my heart." During this state of conviction, he opened the state of his mind to his mother, and requested her prayers. In reply, among other counsels, she advised him to seek the acquaintance of the Rev. John Newton, of St. Mary Woolnoth, London. This was a valuable suggestion. Mr. Newton, as will appear from one of the preceding articles of biography, had himself been in a similar situation to young Bu-

12*

chanan, and therefore knew how to address himself to his mind, and to speak "*a word in season*." Mr. Buchanan now began to attend on Mr. Newton's ministry, but did not immediately find the benefit expected. "But," he observes with genuine humility, "I have now learned how unreasonable was such an early expectation; I have been taught to wait patiently upon God, who waited so long for *me*." In this anxious, mournful condition, he wrote to Mr. Newton. In his letter, he pathetically says, "O sir, what shall I do to inherit eternal life? If the world were my inheritance, I would sell it to purchase that pearl of great price. How I weep when I read of the prodigal son, as described by our Lord! I would walk many miles to hear a sermon from 2d Chronicles, xxxiii. 12, 13." He proceeds, "To-morrow is the day you have appointed for a sermon to young people. Will you remember *me*, and speak some suitable word, that by the aid of the blessed Spirit may reach my heart?" Though this letter was without any signature, it so deeply interested the venerable clergyman to whom it was addressed, that he intimated from the pulpit, that if the writer was present he should be happy to converse with him on the subject of his communication. "I called on him," says Mr. Buchanan, in another letter to his mother, "on the Tuesday following, and experienced such a happy hour as I ought not to forget. If he had been my father, he could not have expressed more solicitude for my welfare."

A great and happy change now took place in the

heart and conduct of this returning penitent. And now he was led once more into the paths of piety, he began again to desire to preach the Gospel. "Yesterday morning," he observes, "I went to hear Dr. S. Near the conclusion of the service, I was insensibly led to admire this passage of the prophet Isaiah, 'How beautiful are the feet of them that preach the Gospel of peace!' It occurred to me that this enviable office was once designed for *me;* that I was called to the ministry, as it were, from my infancy. For my pious grandfather chose me from among my mother's children to live with himself. He adopted me as his own child, and took great pleasure in forming my young mind to the love of God. He warmly encouraged my parent's design of bringing me up to the ministry. I particularly recollect the last memorable occasion of my seeing this good grandfather. The first season of my being at College, I paid him a visit. After asking me some particulars relating to my studies, he put the following question to me; 'What end had I in view in becoming a minister of the Gospel?' I hesitated a moment. But he put an answer into my mouth. 'With a view, no doubt, to the glory of God.' I recollect no other particular of the conversation but this. It made a strong impression upon my mind, and even often recurred to my thoughts in the midst of my unhappy years. It suddenly came into my mind again that I might yet be a preacher of the Gospel. These reflections filled me with delight; and as I walked home, the sensation increased; so that by the time I entered my chamber, my spirits were overpowered, and I fell on my knees before God, and wept. I thought that I, who had experienced so much of the divine mercy, was peculiarly engaged to declare it to others. After fervent prayer, I endeavored to commit myself and my services into the hands of Him who alone is able to direct me." At this period, Mr. Buchanan received a letter from his mother, in which she thus expresses her thankfulness and joy on account of his conversion: "Since you were a boy, it was impressed upon my mind that you would be a good man. I own of late years I was beginning to lose my hope, particularly on the supposition of your going abroad. I thought with myself, this is not God's usual way of bringing sinners to himself. But the word of consolation often came in remembrance, that ' God is a God afar off.' O how merciful has he been to you! What comforting letters have you sent us! Could a thousand pounds a year have afforded an equal consolation? Impossible. It might indeed have tied us faster to the earth, but it could not have set our hearts upon the unsearchable riches that are in Christ Jesus. Your friends at Glasgow are rejoicing with us; some of them saying, ' Had the good old people (meaning his grandfather, and mother) been alive, how this would have revived them!' Among your grandfather's papers I find the inclosed letter, written by Mr. Maculloch to him in a time of distress, when the sins of his youth oppressed him. Read it with care, and may God grant a blessing in the perusal." These sentiments made the penitent very happy. "It is not the smallest of my consolations," he exclaims, "that I have such a mother as this." Through the munificent aid of that benevolent and Christian gentleman, Mr. Henry Thornton, and with the entire approbation of his friend, Mr. Newton, Mr. Buchanan went to the University, where he prosecuted his studies with diligence and piety, and was at length ordained a minister of the Gospel. After preaching for some time in England, he went in a very important situation to India, where, for many years, *he was a burning and shining light, and many rejoiced in his light.*

---

## REV. DR. DWIGHT AND HIS MOTHER.

Timothy Dwight was born at Northampton, in America, May 14th, 1752. His father was a merchant, of good understanding and fervent piety. His mother was the third daughter of Jonathan Edwards, for many years the minister of Northampton, and afterward President of Nassau Hall, well known as one of the ablest divines of the last century. She possessed uncommon powers of mind, and great extent and variety of knowledge. Though married at an early age, and a mother at eighteen, she found time, without neglecting the ordinary cares of her family, to devote herself with the most assiduous attention to the instruction of her numerous children. It was a maxim with her, the soundness of which her own observation through life fully confirmed, that children generally lose several years, in consequence of being considered by their friends as too young to be taught. She pursued a different course with her son: she began to instruct him as soon as he was able to speak; and such was his eagerness,—as well as his capacity for improvement, that he learned the alphabet at a single lesson; and before he was four years old, was able to read the Bible with ease and correctness. With the benefit of his father's example constantly before him, enforced and recommended by the precepts of his mother, he was carefully instructed in the doctrines of religion, as well as in moral duties. She taught him from the very dawn of his reason to fear God, and to keep his commandments; to be conscientiously just, kind, affectionate, charitable, and forgiving; to preserve on all occasions, and under all circumstances, the most sacred regard to truth; and to relieve the distresses, and supply the wants of the poor and unfortunate. She aimed at a very early period to enlighten his conscience, to make him afraid of sin, and to teach him to hope for pardon only through Christ. The impressions thus made upon his mind in infancy were never effaced. A great proportion of the instuction which he received before he arrived at the age of six years, was at home with his mother.

His school-room was the nursery. Here he had his regular hours for study, as in a school; and twice every day she heard him repeat his lesson. Here, in addition to his stated task, he watched the cradle of his younger brothers. When his lesson was recited, he was permitted to read such books as he chose, until the limited period was expired. During these intervals, he often read over the historical parts of the Bible, and gave an account of them to his mother. So deep and distinct was the impression which these narrations then made upon his mind, that their minutest incidents were indelibly fixed upon his memory. His relish for reading was thus early formed, and was strengthened by the conversation and example of his parents. His early knowledge of the Bible led to that ready, accurate, and extensive acquaintance with Scripture, which is so evident in his sermons and writings. At the age of six, he was sent to the grammar-school. Here, for two years, he made rapid advances, when the school was discontinued, so that he returned again to the care of his mother. By this faithful and intelligent guide of his youth, his attention was now directed to geography, history, and other useful studies. *This domestic education rendered him fond of home, of the company of his parents,* and of the conversation of those who were older than himself. Even at this early period of life, while listening to the conversation of his father and friends on the character and actions of the great men of the age—both in the Colonies and in Europe—a deep and lasting impression was made upon his mind ; and he then formed a settled resolution, that he would make every effort in his power to equal those whose talents and character he heard so highly extolled.

In September, 1765, he was admitted as a member of Yale College, where, in 1771, he became a tutor, when he was little more than nineteen years of age. In 1777, he entered into the marriage state, and in the year following, he received the afflicting intelligence of the death of his father. The new and important duties which now devolved upon him, he undertook with great readiness and kindness. He consoled his widowed mother under her painful bereavement, and assisted her in the support and education of the younger children. In this situation, he passed five of the most interesting years of his life; performing, in an exemplary manner, the offices of son, brother, and guardian. He was emphatically the staff and stay of the family. The elder, as well as the younger, were committed to his care, and loved and obeyed him as their father. The filial affection, respect, and obedience which he showed toward his mother, and the more than fraternal kindness with which he watched over the well-being of his brothers and sisters, deserve the most honorable remembrance. To accomplish this object, though destitute of property, he generously relinquished the proportion of the family estate; labored for five years with a diligence and alacrity rarely exampled; and for a long time afterward, he continued his paternal care and liberality. Often did his mother, who died only ten years before him, acknowledge, in language of eloquent affection and gratitude, his kindness, faithfulness, and honorable generosity to her and her children. The respect which she felt and manifested toward him, resembled the affection of a dutiful child toward her father, rather than the feelings of a mother for her son. Well was this invaluable parent repaid for all her care in his religious education, for she declared with joy, a little before her death, that *she did not know the instance in which he ever disobeyed a parental command, or failed in the performance of a filial duty.* As a husband and a father, his life was eminently lovely. The education which he had himself happily received in his youth, he conveyed, as a rich inheritance, to his own children. His highest earthly enjoyment was found at the fireside, in the bosom of his family. To his brothers and sisters, he supplied, as far as possible, the loss they sustained in the death of their worthy father; when that mournful event happened, ten of the children were under twenty-one years of age. For their comfort and support, he superintended the farm, frequently working upon it himself, taught an extensive school, and regularly preached on the Sabbath. For two years, he represented the town of Northampton, in the legislature of the State. In 1783, he became the pastor of a church and congregation at Greenfield, in Connecticut, and remained in that situation till 1795, when, to the sorrow and disappointment of an affectionate people, he entered on the important office of President of Yale College.

This seminary, in which he himself completed his education, was at that time in a languishing and unhappy state. Discipline was relaxed, the number of students was greatly reduced, and what was much worse,

13

many of them had imbibed loose and profane sentiments on the subject of religion, and even went so far
as to assume the names of well-known infidels.    The
President applied himself vigorously to remove this
awful evil.    He boldly met and refuted all the cavils
and arguments of the students, though he gave them
free liberty of debate; and through the smile of Heav-
en on his abilities and faithfulness, infidelity was compelled to flee into its native darkness, and restored
truth appeared in its true dignity and splendor.    His
sound views of the instruction and discipline necessary
for youth will be found in his published works, and
are worthy of serious regard.    From the age of seventeen to sixty-four, he was almost constantly engaged in
the business of education, and during that period, he
had between two or three thousand pupils under his
care.    He presided over the College for more than
twenty years, with honor to himself, and advantage to
the students.    They honored and loved him as a father,
and still revere his memory.    The course of Divinity
which he delivered for their instruction is extensively
circulated in England, and worthy of a cordial recommendation.    For the last few months of his life, he
endured much pain and languor.    His constitution
sunk under incessant application.    His spirit was resigned, his mind serene, and his attachment to the precious truths of revelation more strong and ardent than
ever.    These revived and supported him in the near
prospect of death and eternity.    His conversation, to
the last, was serious, devout, and edifying.    On Sun-

day morning, January 11th, 1817, he bade adieu to
this vale of tears, aged sixty-five. The memory of
this enlightened and useful man is still held in honorable remembrance, and his loss is universally bewailed
as a great public, as well as private calamity.

---

## BARON CUVIER AND HIS MOTHER.

AMONG the many brilliant names that adorn the annals
of modern science, that of Baron Cuvier, the naturalist
and philosopher, ranks pre-eminent. If it be interesting and instructive to trace the windings of a noble
river up to the obscure, and often insignificant spring
from whence it rises, still more interesting and instructive to the contemplative mind must it be to trace back
the history of a great man to his childhood, and to discover the influences that aided in developing his genius,
and the germs of instruction that ultimately expanded
into the rich fruits of knowledge.

The father of Cuvier was advanced in life when he
married a young lady of great virtue and intelligence,
who, on the 22nd of August, 1679, at the town of
Montpelier, became the mother of George Leopold
Cuvier, the subject of our sketch. The loss of a son,
which took place a few months prior to the birth of
George, had such an effect on the health and spirits
of the young mother, that her offspring, at birth, was
so feeble and sickly, that only very faint hopes were
entertained of rearing him. In this respect, his infancy

furnished a parallel to that of a kindred genius, Sir Isaac Newton, and the same extraordinary care and tenderness that distinguished the devoted mother of Newton, was evidenced by the equally admirable mother of Cuvier. With the vigilant eyes of affection, she soon discerned the uncommon powers of mind displayed by her fragile nursling, and while tending his infancy with a care that never relaxed or slumbered, she paid due attention to his early mental cultivation : she piously instilled into his mind the principles of religion, and, it is said, taught him to read fluently by the time he was four years old. Though ignorant of the Latin language, she instructed herself sufficiently to enable her to hear his lessons. Under her superintendence, he commenced and made considerable progress in drawing ; and when his fluctuating health became more established, and he was able to go to school, she conducted him herself to and from the school, and directed his miscellaneous·readings by supplying him with the best works on literature and history. The child so taught and cherished soon acquired a passion for reading, and his evident delight in literary pursuits induced his father to alter his previous determination, in reference to his subsequent pursuits in life.

It had been the intention of the elder Cuvier that his son should adopt the military profession, but fortunately for science, the admirable instruction of the devoted mother had imbued her child with a taste for the more peaceful and ennobling pursuits of literature. The young Cuvier speedily manifested the peculiar

bent of genius as a naturalist, and at fourteen years of
age was appointed president of a society of his school-
fellows, where his oratorical powers were first exercised in discussion on scientific subjects. His fame soon
spread beyond the academy and town where he studied.
And the Duke of Wirtemberg, having heard of his talents and diligence, sent him under his own immediate
patronage, and free of all expense, to the University
of Stuttgard, where he continued four years, with hon-
or to himself, and satisfaction to his friends and pre-
ceptors.

After leaving the University, he passed several years
of his life in studying his favorite subject—natural
history, and made many valuable discoveries that have
conferred immortality on his name. His admirable
mother lived to witness the dawning, but not the meridian greatness of her distinguished son. To a mind
like hers, it must have been a source of unspeakable
consolation that, at a time when infidel principles were
pervading all ranks, and eating like a canker-worm
into the very core of society in France, Cuvier was
true to the hallowed faith that had been taught him
at the holy altar of a mother's knee, and never swerved from the religion whose truths he had lisped in
infancy.

While yet a very young man, Cuvier was elected
President of the National Institute of Paris—an institution that has been celebrated throughout the civilized
world for the learning and ingenuity of its professors.
After the restoration of the Royal Family of France,

13*

in 1818, honors in rich abundance were showered on Cuvier ; but distinctions did not make him relax his diligence, or cease from his favorite pursuits and important discoveries. No less than 206 memoirs of natural objects proceeded from the pen of this distinguished man, added to which, was his constant labor as a lecturer at the Institute, and his unceasing toil in collecting, labeling, and arranging natural curiosities for his immense museum.

While his name is justly dear to men of science, in every relationship of life he was distinguished for his amiability ; and as son, husband, father, citizen, and Christian, commands universal admiration and respect.

---

### REV. LEGH RICHMOND, M.A., AND HIS MOTHER.

LEGH RICHMOND was born at Liverpool, on January 29th, 1772. It was his privilege to have a most estimable mother, endued with a superior understanding, which had been cultivated and improved by an excellent education and subsequent reading, and who, with considerable natural talents and acquirements, manifested a constant sense of the importance of religion.

This affectionate and conscientious parent anxiously instructed him from his infancy in the Holy Scriptures, and in the principles of religion, according to the best of her ability ; a duty which was subsequently well repaid by her son, who became the happy and honored instrument of imparting to his beloved mother clearer and more enlarged views of divine truth than were generally prevalent during the last generation.    It seems highly probable that the seeds of piety were then sown, which, in a future period, and under circumstances of a providential nature, were destined to produce a rich and abundant harvest.

Ye that are mothers, and whose office it more peculiarly is to instill into the minds of your offspring an habitual reverence for God, and a knowledge of the truths of the Gospel, be earnest in your endeavors to fulfill the duties which Providence has assigned to you. and which your tenderness, your affection, and the constant recurrence of favorable opportunities, so admirably fit you to discharge.    Consecrate them to God in early youth; and remember that the child of many prayers can never perish, so long as prayer is availing.    To faith all things are possible, and the promise stands firm,—"I will pour my Spirit on thy seed, and my blessing upon thine offspring."—Isaiah xliv. 3.    Pray, then, for them and with them.    There is an efficacy in the bended knee, in the outstretched hand, in the uplifted heart, in the accents of prayer issuing from the lips of the mother, supplicating God to bless her child, which faith may interpret for its encouragement, and the future shall one day realize.    There is also a solemnity in the act itself, peculiarly calculated to elicit all the best feelings of the heart, and to quicken it in the diligent use of the means best adapted, through divine mercy, to insure the blessing.

Discouragements may arise—impressions that once

excited hope may vanish—the fruit may not be apparent; yet in after times, under circumstances of the most unpromising nature, and scenes, perhaps, of folly, vice, and dissipation, or in the more sober moments of sickness and sorrow, the remembrance of a praying mother may present itself with overwhelming emotion to the heart.   The events of early days may rise up in quick succession before the mind, until the long-lost wanderer, recovered from his slumber of death and sin, may live to be a monument of the pardoning mercy of God, and his last accents be those of gratitude and praise for a pious mother.   This justly celebrated and pious clergyman, whose praise was in all the churches, and whose history is familiar to most readers, died in May, 1828.

---

### H. KIRKE WHITE AND HIS MOTHER.

HENRY KIRKE WHITE was born at Nottingham, on the 21st of March, 1785.  His father, John, was a butcher: his mother, Mary Neville, was of a respectable family, in Staffordshire.  When three years of age he was sent to the school of a Mrs. Garrington, of whom he draws a very pleasing and affectionate picture, in his verses on childhood.

By this good woman he was taught to read; and *by her* his future eminence was very confidently predicted. At six, he was placed under the care of the Rev. John Blanchard, in whose seminary he learnt writing, arithmetic, and French. While here, his love of reading, which had been manifested at a very early age, increased, and though he was employed, when out of school, in carrying the butcher's basket, and was even obliged to devote one whole day in each week to this occupation, yet his progress in his studies was astonishingly rapid. When about seven years of age, he was accustomed to steal into the kitchen for the purpose of teaching the servant to read and write; and for this person he wrote a tale, which he modestly concealed from his mother. In his eleventh year, he one day composed a separate theme for every boy in his class, which consisted of twelve or fourteen scholars, and on this occasion, Mr. Blanchard told them, " that he had never known them write so well before." Some difference, however, between his father and his teachers led to his removal to another school, under the care of Mr. Shipley. To the same cause is to be ascribed a very unworthy representation of his character and disposition, by his former masters; but he soon requited himself of the envy and malignity of this accusation, by various satirical poems, directed against his accusers, in which the rod was applied with a degree of severity and skill which astonished his friends, and galled his enemies. Under his new master, who quickly perceived, and candidly acknowledged his merits, he remained till he was fourteen years of age.

At this stage of our narrative, we cannot avoid calling the attention of our readers to the early exercise of talent on the part of White, chiefly, however, with

the view of remarking, that the great talent he thus
early exhibited, was not merely an occasional display
of genius, a glimmer of fancy, which, in a lucky moment, illumined his path and vanished forever; but
rather the steady labor of a cultivated mind, the result
of unremitting study and constant culture. Love of
knowledge spurred him on, even in boyhood, and led
to a degree of perseverance and industry in his pursuits, which is seldom found in more advanced students. The good effects of this praiseworthy conduct
we would strongly press upon the notice of our young
readers. They establish the important truth too often
neglected, or contemned by the young man of genius,
that, however great may be his natural powers, study
alone can mature them, and lead to their useful exertion.

Among the difficulties which attended the progress
of our young scholar in his literary acquisitions, may
be ranked the difference of opinion which prevailed between his parents on the subject. His father seems at
all times to have looked forward to his following the
same trade as himself, and therefore to have been very
little solicitous about his education. But his mother entertained very different views. She always expressed
the strongest wishes to educate her son in a very superior manner, and was ready to make every effort to secure the necessary means. Her affectionate solicitude
on this point induced her to open a ladies' boarding and
day-school, in Nottingham; and though the profits of
this establishment increased in a very material degree

the means of domestic comfort, yet the wants of rather a numerous family led to large claims on her savings, and when Henry arrived at fourteen years of age, it was resolved to apprentice him to a hosier. Here the term of his misery commenced. He did not relish his new employment, which was not only of the most irksome kind, and too laborious for his tender constitution, but one which left him no time for recreation or study. Hence he was deprived of all that literary enjoyment which could have enabled him to undergo the fatigues of his situation. Constant exertion exhausted him, and vexation and despondency preyed on his mind. It was during this season of wretchedness that he composed his "Address to Contemplation," in which his feelings are very forcibly depicted. At last, after dragging on a miserable existence for a year at the stocking-frame, his fond mother again interposed, and removed him to the office of Messrs. Coldham and Enfield, most respectable attorneys, and town-clerks of Nottingham. His entry took place in 1800, but as no premium could be given with him, he was obliged, as a substitute for it, to serve two years before he was articled.

Henry was now happy. His occupation was congenial to his feelings, and he entered upon its duties with ardor. In that ardor he never relaxed, and though, by the recommendation of his masters, he devoted his leisure hours to the acquisition of the Latin language, and of his own accord engaged in the study of Greek, Italian, Spanish, and Portuguese, he never allowed his fondest pursuits to interfere with his duties to his em-

ployers. His industry was astonishing, and even to
his friends, but partially known. His acquirements in
literature kept pace with his industry, and in a very
short period outstript all expectation. Yet even amidst
these studies, multifarious as they were, he found time
to acquire some knowledge of chemistry and astronomy,
and some skill in drawing, and music, and mechanics.
He attempted to become, and with some difficulty, on
account of his youth, did become a member of a literary
society in his native town, and soon after his election,
according to Southey, "He lectured upon genius, and
spoke extempore, for about two hours, in such a manner, that he received the unanimous thanks of the society, and they elected this young Roscius of oratory
their Professor of Literature." He now began to contribute to several of the periodical works of the day,
particularly the Monthly Mirror, and some of his productions in this miscellany procured him the notice
and friendship of Mr. Capel Lofft, and other literary
gentlemen, who delighted to foster rising genius. Under the sanction of their approbation, he prepared a
volume of poems for the press, and in 1803 published
it, with a dedication to the celebrated Duchess of Dev-
onshire, by whom, however, no notice was ever taken
of the author or his work. In the Monthly Review, a
piece of silly, heartless criticism appeared on the work,
and poor White was stung almost to madness. But
this wanton attack did not produce all the effects which
its dull author seemed to wish, for its malignity and
injustice were so very apparent, that they excited the

notice of Southey, who, during the author's life, was most attentive to his interests, and after his death, recorded his virtues in a memoir, worthy of the high talent of its writer, and of the modest merits of its subject. The attack, too, had been deliberately cruel, for White had informed the critics that the object of his publication was to enable him to prosecute his studies at one of the Universities.

A growing deafness, to which he had been long subject, rendered him incapable of practicing at the bar, and a strong devotional bias inclined him to enter the church.

Henry addressed the editor of the Review on the subject of the critique, and something like the amende honorable appeared in the next number; but still the unkindly wound rankled in the breast of the sensitive poet, and the fear of being thought a just sufferer, induced him afterward to decline a larger publication, projected for his benefit, by Southey, and which, under this distinguished writer's friendly protection, must have prduced a sum equivalent to the author's wants.

When the corporeal defect before alluded to was found to affect his prospects of success at the bar, it became necessary to choose another profession for him; and after considerable deliberation, it was resolved that he should enter the church. Hitherto, his attention had been directed to religious studies, and his notions on the various systems of belief prevalent in England do not seem to have been settled. Like many youthful speculators, indeed, Deism, or something approach-

14

ing to it, appears to have been his first creed; but he soon learned to correct his opinions, and to form them on the standard of truth, furnished by the Scriptures. With the characteristic ardor of his mind, he was now anxious to qualify himself for promulgating his religious belief to others, and after encountering many obstacles, he seemed at last almost certain of entering the University of Cambridge, under the auspices of Mr. Simeon, of St. John's College, to whom he had been introduced, and by whom his worth was highly appreciated. Preparatory to this step, his employers, who had most kindly agreed to relinquish the latter, and to them the most valuable half of his services, gave him leave of absence for a few weeks, to enable him to study, and recruit his health, by a change of air. He retired, accordingly, to his favorite spot, the village of Wilford, at Clifton Woods, where, at the end of little more than a month, he had the mortification to learn that the plans formed for his benefit had entirely failed. The effects of this disappointment on his mind are best described by his own pen:—

> " There fell my hopes,—I lost my all in this,
> My cherished all of visionary bliss ;
> Now hope farewell, farewell all joys below :
> Now welcome sorrow, and now welcome woe."

His health, too, suffered severely, and his constitution received a shock from which it never recovered. It is true he returned to Nottingham, and to his legal studies, with fresh vigor, determined to make up by redoubled assiduity the time he had lost. But his disappointment preyed on his mind, and his struggles were those of despair. In the course of a very short period, however, the exertions of his friends, and the kindness of Mr. Simeon, revived his hopes, and with these his health; and so effectually did the latter gentleman employ his influence, that he not only procured for him a Sizarship in St. John's College, but obtained other assistance, without which the young scholar could not have profited by the situation thus conferred on him. Mr. Simeon did not stop even here; he interested himself in his young friend's improvement and general conduct, advised him to decline the aid offered to him by the Elland Clerical Society, and recommended him to place himself under the tuition of the Rev. Mr. Grainger, of Winteringham, for a year, that he might appear at college with greater advantagê.

Everything being now arranged to his satisfaction, Henry left Nottingham in October, 1804, and repaired to the house of his tutor, under whom he pursued his studies for twelve months, with the greatest perseverance and success. His amiable qualities procured him the friendship of Mr. Grainger during his life, and an affectionate testimonial of his worth after his death.

Well might this gentleman boast of his pupil, for his attainments as a scholar were the admiration of all who knew him. Accordingly, when he entered college, his classical knowledge was perceived to be of the most respectable kind, and an unremitting application to study added daily to his literary stores.

A scholarship soon became vacant, and he spent his days and nights in preparing himself to become a candidate for it. But his health sunk alarmingly under these exertions, and after all, he was obliged to decline the competition.

The general examination followed, and believing it to be essential to his future progress, that on this occasion he should at all events confirm, and if possible, excel his previous reputation, he renewed his exertions in the midst of indisposition and weakness; and though limited to a fortnight to prepare himself for what had occupied the attention of others during the whole term, and obliged on the six days of examination to support himself by strong medicines, he persevered in his purpose, and obtained the object of his ambition :—" He was pronounced the first man of his year." But the honor was dearly purchased—life was the price he was to pay.

To repair his shattered health, he now took a journey to London, but the effect was not favorable to him. On his return to College, therefore, he was advised to relax a little in his studies ; but how little he did in reality relax, will be apparent from the following mode in which he arranged the labors of each day :—" Rise at half past five. Devotions and walk till seven. Chapel and breakfast till eight. Study and lecture till one. Four and a half clear reading. Walk, etc., and dinner, and Woollaston, and chapel, to six. Six to nine, reading, the hours nine to ten, devotions. Bed at ten."

In the exercises of this year, he was highly successful. He was again pronounced the first at the great College examination, and one of the three best theme writers. He was set down as a medalist, and expected to take a senior Wrangler's degree. He excited the highest hopes throughout the whole University, and every honor seemed to be within his reach. He was flattered by the distinction conferred on him—his ambition prompted him to excel—and though his days were full of pain, and his nights sleepless and agitating, he still pursued his studies with increasing assiduity.

The consequences were such as might have been anticipated—the little health left to him perceptibly declined, and he was sunk in mind, to the very depth of wretchedness. When the long vacation arrived, he again visited London; but the kindness of his college, having provided him with a tutor during this interval, he neither relaxed from his studies, nor suffered himself to enjoy the quiet of retirement, or his mother's home. On his return to college, therefore, he was in a worse state than when he left it. His frame was now totally shaken, and his mind appeared to be worn out. His great anxiety was to conceal his situation from his mother and brother, and while enduring agony, he was holding out to them hopes of amendment. His brother, however, was informed of his danger by a friend, and hastened to Cambridge, but when he arrived he found Henry delirious. The unhappy youth recovered sufficiently to know him for a few

14*

moments; the next day he sunk into a stupor, and on Sunday, 19th of October, 1806, expired. It was the opinion of his physicians that if he had lived, his intellects would have been affected. He was buried in All Saints' Church, Cambridge, where a monument, sculptured by Chantrey, has been erected to his memory by Mr. Francis Booth, of Boston, in America.

The following lines evince his high attachment to his beloved mother, whose spirit was so congenial with his own:

### TO MY MOTHER.

And canst thou, mother, for a moment think
That we, thy children, when old age shall shed
Its blanching honors on thy weary head,
Could from our best of duties ever shrink ?
Sooner the sun from his high sphere should sink,
Than we, ungrateful, leave thee in that day,
To pine in solitude thy life away,
Or shun thee, tottering on the grave's cold brink.
Banish the thought !—where'er our steps may roam,
O'er smiling plains, or wastes without a tree,
Still will fond memory point our hearts to thee,
And paint the pleasures of thy peaceful home ;
While duty bids us all thy griefs assuage,
And smooth the pillow of thy sinking age.

-----

## THE MOTHER OF LUCRETIA AND MARGARET DAVIDSON.

MODERN literary biography contains no account more intensely interesting than the affecting records of the lives and writings of Lucretia and Margaret Davidson

—two gifted American girls, sisters—whose astonishing genius, exhibited in early childhood, and whose sweet dispositions and youthful piety rendered their brief lives full of pleasing and profound instruction. The elder sister, Lucretia, was a remarkably precocious child, learning to read almost without any instruction; and what was far more remarkable, teaching herself to write before any of her family supposed her able to pen a letter. She learned to write, it seems, in order that she might put down her thoughts; and at the age of six or seven, covered many sheets of paper with poetical compositions before any one suspected the nature of her private employment, or knew of her being able to use her pen. The loss of the missing writing paper, consumed by Lucretia, led to a discovery, which covered the modest, trembling child with confusion, but filled the heart of her fond and anxious mother with delight. Every year from this early age was marked by great mental improvement, and a continuance of the faculty of composition—extraordinary in one so young—elegant poems full of fine thoughts, finely expressed, abounding in affection, moral purity, and religious feeling—flowed from her pen in rich abundance. The health of this gifted creature was very delicate, and probably the mind was too active for its earthly tenement. At the age of seventeen, after a lingering illness, she died, leaving the remembrance of her youthful piety and radiant genius, as a consolation to her bereaved family and friends.

What renders the above account more remarkable,

is the fact, that, at the time Lucretia Davidson died, there was an infant sister in the family, named Margaret, then not more than two and a half years old. This child, remarkable almost from birth for vivacity and intelligence, seemed to inherit all her sister's genius, sanctified in a yet more peculiar manner by the subsequent knowledge of that sister's early death, and a constant listening to, and perusal of her writings. Margaret had a greater degree of precocity than was displayed even by Lucretia. Of her it might literally be said, "She lisped in numbers, for the numbers came." She also wrote on many graceful themes with a melody of versification and spiritual elevation of thought and feeling, that will ever render her name remarkable among the good and gifted of her country. The lives of these sweet sisters were parallels of each other; alike in person, early development, similarity of taste and pursuits, and alike also in the brevity of their mortal career. Margaret had not attained quite to the age at which Lucretia died, when she also was called to resign life, and all its allurements, and opening prospects of usefulness and literary distinction. But faith triumphed over earthly longings and human affections, enabling her to resign herself to the will of her heavenly Father, of whose mercy in Christ Jesus she was fully assured.

Such is a brief outline of the lives of these two lovely sisters. Two of the most distinguished names in American literature have thought it a labor of love to write their lives and edit their poems—Miss Sedgewick has presented the public with the life of Lucretia, and more recently Washington Irving has written the life of Margaret. The inquiry naturally arises, What were the influences that aided in developing, and rightly directing, such extraordinary minds? The genius of these sweet sisters was the rich and gracious gift of God. Its training, development, and purity of aim, was the important work of their admirable mother.

Mrs. Margaret Davidson is the wife of a physician, Dr. Oliver Davidson, a lover of science, and a man of intellectual tastes. It seems that the delicacy of constitution, which both her daughters exhibited, was to be expected from the circumstance, that Mrs. Davidson was nearly always an invalid. Yet, while possessing existence on terms of frequent pain and suffering, this devoted mother made her sick-bed a hallowed shrine, where her children could receive constant instruction in piety and patience, both by precept and example.

Possessed of fine talents, warm sympathies, and a great love of the beautiful, both in nature and art, it is not wonderful that she should have sympathized in the pursuits of her gifted daughters—watched with pleased surprise the early development of their minds, and early instilled those principles of religion, without which genius is but a fatal gift to its possessor, and a fearful power let loose upon society. Washington Irving says, in reference to her instruction of her daughter Margaret,—" That it was one poetical mind ministering to another."

There was much prudence and correct judgment exhibited by Mrs. Davidson in the early management

of her remarkable children. She did not allow her
own appreciation of their talents to lead her to stimu-
late them unwisely, either by praise, or other injurious
excitements. She saw that to repress, in some cases,
their ardor in the pursuit of their studies, was absolutely necessary. Thus, Lucretia, during a long illness,
was her mother's only attendant, and her great talents
were very wisely not permitted to exempt her from
the humbler duties that devolve upon her sex and
station. These temporary suspensions of her studies,
so far from retarding her progress, only sent her to
them with increased freshness and ardor; and, while
there cannot be a doubt that the activity of this sweet
child's mind wore out her fragile frame, yet all that
judicious maternal care could do to preserve this delicate plant was tried. And in Margaret's case, warned
by the early death of Lucretia, the utmost anxiety was
manifested by Mrs. Davidson to prevent, if possible,
the too early mental development of Margaret. With this
view she was not taught to read early, and writing implements were kept out of her way; but nothing could
damp or repress her genius; she composed solemn
stanzas, during the severe storms that sometimes visit
that climate, before she had ever read a line of poetry—
observed all the beautiful phenomena of nature by
which she was surrounded on the shores of Lake
Champlain, and made it the subject of her early verse.
It was found impossible to check this strong propensity of nature; nevertheless, at a subsequent period,
after Margaret had made considerable progress in her
education, symptons of weakness appearing that alarm-

ed the watchful mother, she exerted her authority, and made it a request that Margaret should lay aside the pen and books, and devote her time to healthful exercise and recreation. This was a sore trial of obedience; but Margaret submitted to her mother's will, and persevered in the course prescribed, until it was found that her health actually suffered by it; and when the restriction was taken off, and she was allowed to return to her literary pursuits, her health for a season improved.

Nothing was more beautiful in the character of Mrs. Davidson, than the resignation she evinced when successively bereaved, after long years of anxiety, of these extraordinary children. To lose such daughters was a more than ordinary trial; particularly when it is remembered that the fond mother was an invalid, as drooping and fragile (though more tenacious of life) as her children. That she possessed a highly sensitive temperament, which must have deepened her anguish at the loss she sustained; yet, though she mourned her bereavement with all the tenderness of a fond mother, she was enabled to look up to her heavenly Father with the piety of a Christian, and to acquiesce in His wise arrangements without a murmur, though with many tears.

As soon as her health and spirits recovered from the shock inflicted by Margaret's death, she set herself to collect her daughter's poems, and select from them those most suited to meet the public eye. Appended to the beautiful sketch by Washington Irving of Margaret Davidson's life, they form a volume fitted to appear beside the life and literary remains of Lucretia.

The following beautiful lines from Lucretia to her mother are such a sweet epitome of maternal love, that they must find their way to every heart.

### TO MY MOTHER.

WRITTEN IN LUCRETIA'S SIXTEENTH YEAR.

Oh ! thou, whose care sustained my infant years,
   And taught my prattling lip each note of love ;
Whose soothing voice breathed comfort to my fears,
   And round my brow hope's brightest garland wove—

To thee my lay is due, the simple song,
   Which nature gave me at life's opening day ;
To thee these rude, these untaught strains belong,
   Whose heart indulgent will not spurn my lay.

Oh ! say, amid this wilderness of life,
   What bosom would have throbbed like thine for me ?
Who would have smiled responsive ?   Who, in grief,
   Would e'er have felt, and feeling, grieved like thee ?

Who would have guarded with a falcon eye
   Each trembling footstep, or each sport of fear ?
Who would have marked my bosom bounding high,
   And clasped me to her heart with love's bright tear ?

Who would have hung around my sleepless couch,
   And fanned with anxious hand my burning brow ?
Who would have fondly pressed my fevered lip,
   In all the agony of love and woe ?

None but a mother—none but one like thee,
   Whose bloom had faded in the midnight watch ;
Whose eye, for me, has lost its witchery,
   Whose form has felt disease's mildewed touch.

Yes ! thou hast lighted me to health and life,
   By the bright lustre of thy youthful bloom—
Yes, thou hast wept so oft o'er every grief,
   That woe hath traced thy brow with marks of gloom.

Oh, then, to thee, this rude and simple song,
  Which breathes of thankfulness and love for thee;
To thee, my mother, shall this lay belong,
  Whose life is spent in toil and care for me.

---

## MRS. MARTHA RAMSAY AND HER CHILDREN.

SOON after this lady became a mother, she studied with much interest most of the popular and practical works which treated of education, both in the French and English language, that she might be well informed of the nature of the new duties she was called to perform. Her favorite authors on this subject seem to have been Locke and Dr. Witherspoon. The object she had in view was to attain for her children a well-regulated mind, and a healthy constitution. To secure health of body, they were early accustomed to expose themselves to all the varieties of their native climate.

To favor the former object, they were taught to subject their passions to the control of reason and religion —to subdue their tempers—to practice self-denial—to endure disappointment, and to resist temptations to pleasure ; above all, her children were the subject of prayer, even before they saw the light. With one exception, she devoted them all to God in baptism, publicly in the midst of the congregation, rejoicing thus openly to declare her faith in the Christian religion, and her respect for all its institutions. Such a mother failed not early to impart to her beloved little ones the knowledge of the doctrines of the Gospel. She enjoined

15

them by precept, but most of all by her own pious example, to read a portion of the Holy Scriptures daily—to prize them as the standard of faith and rule of action, as a message from God of eternal importance, to be believed, loved, and obeyed. Learning from this blessed book, that "foolishness is bound up in the heart of a child, but that the rod of correction shall drive it thence," she, on proper occasions, but always with judgment and discretion, sometimes with prayer, and often with tears, but never with anger, made a due use of the rod.

As her children advanced in years, she carried her sons through a course of education, fitting them for entering college; and with the assistance of a valued and accomplished friend, she conducted the several studies of her daughters at home. As mistress of her own family, she never omitted the duty of instructing her domestics, by reading the Scriptures with them, and engaging in prayer; and on Sunday, in addition to her own family, the young slave children connected with them were also instructed by means of catechetical lessons. In cases of temporary separation, deliverances, or other providences, or even misconduct, or quarrels, she had recourse with the parties concerned to a throne of grace.

As a mother, she was moderate in urging her parental rights, allowing her children every indulgence compatible with their best interests; participating in their sports—amusing their solitude—and dropping the character of the mother in that of the companion and friend.

These observations will be fully illustrated in the following extract, given from one of her letters to her eldest son:

*September 11th,* 1810.

DEAR DAVID:

I wrote to you not long ago, telling you of the departure of my dear Miss Futerell. Her absence makes everything desolate with me, and your sisters more than sympathize with me, for in addition to mine, they feel their own sorrow. I have in them, however, this consolation, that, by every act of their lives, they show how much they have profited by her advice and example: never were parents more blessed than your father and I, in daughters; and I hope God will return seventy-fold into their bosoms the comfort they give to ours.

Your time of vacation is drawing on. I trust you are not losing your time for study, and that as you grow older, you are resisting every propensity to idleness or folly of any kind. Your judgment must be well informed. You have lived from infancy within the sound of good advice; and although some dispositions are restive under any advice that clashes with their present gratification, I flatter myself you have a more ingenuous disposition, and that no effort on the part of your parents and friends, to make you wiser and better, will be lost upon you.

Dr. Keith gave us, yesterday, an excellent sermon on these words: — "Who can understand his errors? Cleanse thou me from secret faults." We ought, dear child, to take great pains to understand our errors; we have, every one, by nature, some secret error, some constitutional defect or vice. In childhood, the advice or authority of parents may restrain it; still it is there. As we grow older, we must watch for ourselves, restrain ourselves—look up to God for help, while we exercise such acts of self-denial as shall break the bias, and keep it from producing a vicious habit, which, alas! may become too strong for us, and be our curse and our master as long as we live. Persons about your time of life are apt to think themselves very wise, and to pay very slender attention to the voice of their superiors: this is a very great error; as, by such conduct, they not only deprive themselves of the experience of those older and wiser than themselves, but they appear, and really are, very unlovely in their tempers to those who reprove or advise them, whether parents or others. At your time of life, every false appearance of pleasure is taken for a reality, and the restraints of virtuous industry and hard study a burden too heavy to be borne. May God give you wisdom to understand your errors, and a manly resolution to resist every temptation to evil; make you lovely in your temper, diligent in the pursuits of useful science, and enable you, by conciliatory and engaging manners, to make friends to yourself among the wise and good, wherever you go.

## THE REV. WILLIAM THORP AND HIS MOTHER.

THE Rev. William Thorp was for many years a most useful and eminently pious minister of the Gospel, at Bristol. The home influences that developed his character, and turned his mind toward religion, were very impressive and powerful: his own description furnishes a most affecting and deeply interesting account of his admirable mother, to whom no other pen than his own could do equal justice. In a sermon preached at the Tabernacle, Moorfields, March 16th, 1828, on the subject of the beneficial effects of affliction, from the words—"We know that all things work together for good to them that love God, to them who are the called according to his purpose"—Romans viii. 28—the Rev. W. Thorp introduced the following tribute to his mother's memory, and bright example of that mother's faith.

"The words of the text are doubtless intended for the common benefit of the Christian church; but I have looked upon them, likewise, as a family heritage. It was the favorite text of my venerated father, who found in it consolation and support, in the course of a difficult and laborious ministry. It was no less dear to the heart of my mother, who used to quote it in her easy-chair, and on her pillow of rest. When the weight of affliction overcame her feelings in the hours of trial, then she used to say, 'Let me sit down and rest myself, for "we know that all things work togeth-

15*

er for good to them that love God, to them who are
the called according to his purpose." ' My father was
removed in the middle of his pious career, and in the
vigor of his manhood, leaving behind him little of the
goods of this earth, but leaving a large and uneducated family. My mother was then confined in childbed, having been delivered the day before my father
expired. The last words uttered by him to my mother, in this distressing situation, were, ' Call the child
Christiana.' ' All things must work together for good
to them that love God.' To make the measure full, it
happened that all the rivers of the neighborhood were
overflowing at that season, causing on all sides incon-
venience, damage, and distress. Contemplate, then,
for a moment, I beseech you, this scene of domestic
calamity! My father, the supporter of us all, dead!
My mother confined in childbed,—a numerous family
of little children clinging round her, and the water a
foot deep in the ground-floor of the house! Still she
always affirmed that the happiest season of her life
was this season of calamity, in which she derived the
fullness of consolation from the words of our text: so
that when, a few days after my father had been carried to his place of rest, our house was robbed of
everything that could be borne away, and also of the
last quarter's salary which my mother had received,—
when, then, having discovered our loss, my eldest sister ran breathless into her mother's chamber, exclaiming, ' Mother, the thieves have stolen all we had in
this world! w▬▬his also work for good ?' The Chris-

tian replied : ' Yes ! for " we know that all things work
together for good to them that love God :" ' and the
result justified her confidence."

It is not surprising that such a bright example of
piety and faith, in circumstances of such deep affliction,
should have made a powerful impression on the mind
of her son.   And when we see him afterward a faithful minister of Christ—diligent, and successful in his
holy calling, and behold him the subject of many painful trials and bereavements, all borne with hallowed
Christian resignation, we behold the result of such a
mother's prayers and example, in the excellence and
usefulness of her son.

## MISS JANE TAYLOR AND HER MOTHER.

JANE and her sister spent a part of every day with
their father, receiving from him the rudiments of their
education; but a considerable part with their mother,
who, from the first, made her daughters her companions
—treating them and conversing with them as reasona-
ble beings.   They were accustomed to attend, and to
assist her in every domestic engagement, learning at
once the reason and the practice of all that was done.
In the afternoon and evening, while employed by their
mother's side, subjects of all kinds, within the range of
their comprehension, were discussed.   These conversations were at intervals relieved by singing hymns—a
practice which tends, insensibly, to b▪▪▪▪ll the best

and happiest emotions of the infant heart with the language of piety.

It was especially the practice of their mother, in her treatment of her children, to avoid everything like manœuvring or mystery, as well as all unnecessary concealment of the reasons of her conduct toward them. She confided in them as friends; and at the earliest time at which such ideas could enter their minds, they were acquainted with their father's affairs; so far, at least, as was necessary to qualify them to sympathize in every care, and to induce them to adapt their own feelings and expectations to their parent's means. This plan, moreover, preserved them, as far as children can be preserved, from the temptation to practice those petty artifices which debase the mind, and benumb the conscience.

As it formed the material part of Jane's intellectual education, I may here mention a custom adopted by her mother a year or two before the time of which I am now speaking—that of reading aloud at every meal. Her hearing being so far defective as to prevent her from freely taking part in conversation, she had recourse to a book, that the social hours might not be seasons of silence. By constant use, she acquired the habit of taking her food with little interruption to the reading; and only on occasions of extreme ill health was it ever wholly suspended. This practice, while it was a solace and delight to herself, and in some degree enabled her to forget her misfortune in being shut out from free intercourse with her family—to them proved, directly and indirectly, highly beneficial, especially in preventing unprofitable conversation, in cherishing a literary taste, and in imparting, without labor or cost of time, a great mass of information :—and the choice of books was always made with a view to the pleasure and advantage of the younger members of the family.

------

## WILLIAM KNIBB AND HIS MOTHER.

THE present age is pre-eminently distinguished by its Missionary spirit. The Christian church, rousing itself from the slumber of ages, has in the nineteenth century yielded obedience to the divine commission, "Go ye therefore and teach all nations." As this labor of love is the most difficult that the Christian can undertake, it follows that the character of the Christian missionary often exhibits faith and moral courage in their purest and noblest forms. Among the many distinguished heroes of the cross who have visited dangerous climes, and more dangerous savage tribes of the human family, no name ranks higher than that of WILLIAM KNIBB. It is a pleasing and encouraging fact that his childhood was passed and his habits formed under the hallowed influence of maternal piety.

Mr. Knibb was born at Kettering, in Northamptonshire, on the 17th of September, 1803. His mother was a woman of very extraordinary piety and intelligence. She was unwearied in implanting the seeds of divine truth in his infant mind. His nurses and little hymns were lisped at her knee, and she was careful to instruct him, not only in the words, but the meaning of the sweet lessons that she taught him. It was the lot of this distinguished woman to have two sons engage in the arduous labors of a missionary life. Her eldest son, Thomas, was the companion of William, at the Sunday-school of Mr. Toller's meeting-house, at Kettering. Thomas went out, early in life, to Jamaica, and was soon called to receive the reward of his labors in the mansions of eternal bliss. William, at the age of fourteen, was apprenticed to a printer, with whom he removed to Bristol, where he gave such evidence of the good effects of his pious mother's early instruction, that he was received into the church at Broadmead, being baptized by the venerable Dr. Ryland. When the intelligence of his brother Thomas' death reached England, William offered to supply his place. He was accepted by the Baptist Missionary Society, and forthwith set sail for Jamaica. The state of society in Jamaica, at the time William Knibb commenced his labors there, was depraved beyond description. Slavery, in all its moral and physical horrors, polluted alike the oppressed and their oppressors. With a zeal that never tired, and a courage that never quailed, Knibb denounced the fearful system, and though the subject of much persecution, his labors never flagged until he had the unspeakable happiness of beholding the fetters of the oppressed negro broken. His success as an ambassador of the cross was wonderful. Myriads learned of him the way of salvation, and the faithful and affec-

tionate colored people among whom he labored felt
for their devoted pastor an attachment and gratitude,
and exhibited as a church a zeal and liberality, which
few European churches could parallel, and none could
exceed.

In his speeches, Mr. Knibb was often known to re-
vert to the period of his childhood, and to the lessons
of pious lore his admirable mother had taught him.
No one who had enjoyed the privilege of hearing William Kinbb speak or preach, could fail to be impressed
with the earnest manliness of his style, the command-
ing dignity of his person, the fearless energy of his
sentiments, and the all-pervading tone of pure evangelical piety that he evinced.   And when news recently
reached England that the full tones of that fine voice
were silent in the grave, that in the vigor of meridian
manhood that noble head was laid low in the tomb,
it required all the fortitude that religion inspires to
prevent the rebellious wish, that his span had been
lengthened, from rising in the heart.   But while this
was the first feeling in the minds of others, no shadow
of gloom or discontent dimmed the brightness of the
last hours of William Knibb.   He died of fever, after
a short illness, in the 42nd year of his age.   His last
sermon was from the words, "The glorious Gospel of
the blessed God, which was committed to my trust."
—1 Tim. i. 11.   "A trust" whose injunctions he had
fulfilled with a more than ordinary degree of faithfulness.   There is a beautiful incident recorded of his
death-bed ; a brother, who was watching by him, repeated Cowper's lines :

> "Behind a frowning Providence,
> He hides a smiling face."

The dying Christian exclaimed, "Oh yes, brother, it is so, but what bliss to see the cloud dispersed, and the smile of God resting upon *me!*" The sense of this divine, approving smile, so irradiated the dark valley of the shadow of death, that the dying chamber of William Knibb was emphatically the vestibule of heaven. Oh, when such a life, crowned by such a death, are viewed as the results (under the divine blessing) of maternal influence rightly exerted, we would point every mother to the bright example, and say, "Go thou and do likewise." We cannot conclude this article without presenting a most delightful exhibition of

### KNIBB'S FILIAL AFFECTION.

"After one of the jubilee services at Kettering, when the multitude had been thrilled with his eloquence, Knibb found me talking with friends, and, placing his arm within mine, said, 'Stovel, I want you to go with me to my mother's grave—will you go?' 'With all my heart,' was the reply; and with another friend, we walked together up the street, toward the church-yard. As we passed along, he stopped suddenly where the main roads cross in the town, and directed my attention to a window on a second floor, looking down the street to where we stood. 'There,' he said, 'do you see that window with the muslin blind?' I replied, 'Yes.' 'Well,' he said, 'my mother lived there when I left her. We had parted, and I had come down into the street here to go to Jamacia, to take charge of my brother's school, who was dead. She put her head out of the window, and called after me: " William! William! mind, William, I had rather hear that you had perished in the sea, than that you had dishonored the society you go to serve." I never forgot those words—they were written on my heart.' We passed on, talking of the effects which such a sentiment had in fostering his courage and zeal at different periods of his trial and labor. As we ascended the rising path which slopes down the side into the street, when drawing near to the gate of the church-yard, he stopped and said, ' How unchanged the things are! That stone stands at the side of the path just as it did when I used to strike my marbles against it. See, they used to bound and roll down there.' On entering the grave-yard, he became filled with awe, and walking up to his mother's grave, he stood as if in the act of worship, and after a while said, ' There she lies. See, there's her name. She died Jan. 25, 1835. She was such a mother! I wish my children were here, Stovel, to sprinkle some flowers on her grave.' His expressions were calm, and at considerable intervals. My attention was fixed on him; and the thing which struck me most forcibly, was the fact, that in minds which are suited to great and daring actions, the main spring lies in these sensibilities of the heart, which are kindled and augmented by domestic piety."—*Stovel's Funeral Sermon.*

16

### REV. THEOPHILUS LESSEY AND HIS MOTHER.

It was the lot of the pious and talented subject of our present sketch to lose his estimable mother during his early childhood, before he could appreciate either the value of her character, or the magnitude of his loss. Still, it is an evidence of the tenacity of early recollections, and the influence of example, even in the first years of life, that the character of Theophilus Lessey was a transcript of that of his mother. Mrs. Lessey suffered much from delicate health, and also from domestic bereavements. Her husband, the Rev. Theophilus Lessey, was a minister in the Wesleyan Connexion; their union subsisted seventeen years, and they had several children, many of whom, after much suffering, they were called to resign. The childhood of the young Theophilus was marked by extreme delicacy of frame and constitution; and the frequent illness of his devoted mother, with the circumstances of his infant brother's sickness and death, could not fail to make a deep impression on the mind of a thoughtful, observant child. This impression was deepened by the pious conversation of his mother, which led his young mind to think of Him in whose hands are the issues of life.

Soon after he had completed his eighth year, he was deprived by death of his estimable mother, a loss which he always deplored; and many years after, when he was writing a memoir of his father's valuable life, he says of the mother he so early lost, " She was eminently pious, and wholly devoted to God; I may be allowed to say that, although my recollection of her is faint, and at the early age at which it pleased God to deprive me of so dear and valued a parent, I was not capable of estimating the great worth of her character, yet I shall never forget those exercises of maternal piety which tenderly interested my infant heart. Frequently has she taken my sister and myself to her, and talked to us in the most affecting manner on the nature and importance of religion.  Such conversations generally terminated in fervent prayer in our behalf.

" Her friends, also, have often testified to me the high veneration in which she was held by all with whom she was intimately acquainted.   But she was the child of affliction, and called to glorify God rather by patient submission than active exertion."

Such was the mother whose piety, like a ray of light, irradiated the mind of her child, and lingered there until, by the blessing of God, that mind, with all the enthusiasm of youth, kindled with a fervor of piety that made him a most valuable and successful preacher of the everlasting Gospel of Christ.  He ultimately rose to great eminence in the Wesleyan Connexion, filling the important office of President of the Conference, in the year 1839.  The Conference over which he presided was remarkable for the solemn and devout celebration of the Centenary of Wesleyan Methodism, and it was on this account, especially, one of the most memorable ever known.

In the midst of the labors of this faithful servant of God, he was arrested by a severe attack of pulmonary disease, which, though at first it partially yielded to medical treatment, was unsubdued, and after a long period of suffering, borne with the utmost Christian resignation, his life was brought somewhat suddenly to a close, on Thursday, 10th of June, 1841, in the fifty-fifth year of his age, and the thirty-third of his ministry.

It is an affecting fact, that, on the day of his death, a very few hours prior to that event, he mentioned his mother, and even then expressed his deep sense of that early loss. So true it is that first impressions are very often last impressions. How necessary, then, that they should be right impressions!

---

## RECOLLECTIONS OF A MOTHER BY HER ELDER SON.

THE days of my childhood have long since passed away; but the remembrance of them, though sometimes mingled with sadness, is often soothing and refreshing to my spirit. The recollections of an honored, intelligent, affectionate, and pious mother I love most to cherish, because they not only delight, but elevate and purify my heart. From the earliest dawnings of intellect and affection, my attachment to her was strong, and her influence unbounded. Nor did they diminish with my advancing childhood and youth; for they were sustained and strengthened by a tenderness, a prudence, and a piety, the most uniform and watchful. Even now I seem, at times, to feel the gentle movements of my kind and anxious mother, as, amid the shivering cold of a northern winter, she came night after night to my lowly bed, long after my eyes were closed in sleep, and scarcely waked me from my slumber, while she carefully pressed the warm covering around my feet and limbs.

Nor can I soon forget the impression oft made upon my childish heart, when the door of the sitting-room opened upon me, while engaged with my morning's book or play, and I looked up and saw my mother enter, with her Bible in her hands, and her face still wet with her tears. I needed none to tell me what had been her employment, or whence she came. More than once, in the pursuit of her I loved, I had followed her to the place of her retirement, found her upon her knees, and listened to her tones of fervent tenderness, while, with many tears, she prayed God to have mercy upon me and keep me from evil, and to bless those she loved. On such occasions—kneeling or standing beside my praying mother—I had a strange but affecting sense of a present God, who heard her prayer, and thought and felt that I could not, must not grieve or disobey such a tender, godly mother.

When some ten or eleven years of my life had rolled quietly away, I was thrown, at school, into the company of boys who did not fear to take God's name in vain, and learned to imitate their examples so far as to

16*

use improper, if not profane language. My ever watchful mother soon learned my danger and my sin, and calling me privately to a seat by her side, warned and reproved me with a grief and tenderness which I could not resist. She reminded me that she had dedicated me to God in baptism, and even before my birth had devoted me to his service ; that I was the Lord's child. Punishment I could, perhaps, have borne, but her words and her tears broke my heart, though proud and rebellious. She made me feel that I had sinned against a good and holy God, and that my wickedness was greatly increased, because of the vows which were upon me, and because she had so often consecrated me to God. I felt ashamed and distressed that I had wounded a heart so pious and so affectionate, and probably while memory lasts I shall never forget the time and the place, the expressive countenance, and the earnest manner of my mother.

From my earliest childhood I had been taught, and in some degree accustomed, to pray, and now began seriously to seek the salvation of my soul. In my mother I had confidence, and from her I sought counsel. As she lay upon her sick-bed she turned to me and said, with a seriousness of manner, and with a tone of emotion which impressed the words upon my inmost soul, "Strive, my son, agonize, to enter in at the strait gate." Before my thirteenth year I was permitted, with others of my own age, to approach the table of the Lord, and took upon myself those baptismal vows of consecration to God, which had been often present to my heart and conscience.

My mind had been sometimes powerfully impressed by the fervor and tenderness of my mother's prayers, when she assembled her children around the family altar, and supplicated the protection and blessing of God upon us and our absent father. Now I was more deeply affected when on a similar occasion my mother turned to me and said, "Henceforth, my son, we shall expect you to lead the devotions of the family in your father's absence." In the following year I left the home of my childhood, to pursue my studies in a distant city, and was afterward only an occasional inmate in my father's house. But my mother's influence, the remembrance of her example and prayers, still followed me, as a guardian angel, to preserve me from the many dangers and temptations which were around my path.

During one of my college vacations I was called to take charge of my father's school. After two or three days I was somewhat tried by the misconduct of several boys but little younger than myself, and at dinner gave vent to my feelings by the remark, "I do not know but I shall have to kill some of those boys." My mother turned upon me her full, dark eyes, kindled and yet softened by the emotions of her soul, and twice repeating my name, with a look and a tone strongly expressive of surprise and grief, conveyed to my heart gently, but effectually, the deserved rebuke. I soon sought my chamber, there to weep over my impatient spirit, and to ask forgiveness for my sin against God, and my unkindness to my mother.

During the years that have since glided swiftly away, I have ever felt myself more indebted to my mother than to any other human being for whatever I have attained or enjoyed. The remembrance of her instructions and reproofs still excites me to be consistent, more happy, as a disciple and a minister of Jesus Christ, and I praise God that she yet lives to bless me with her counsel, her example, and her prayers. Nor has the blessing been confined to myself; all my brothers and sisters, except my youngest brother, have become pious, as we trust, in very early life. May very many who read the "Mothers of the Wise and Good," through its influence, and by the abundant grace of God, become such blessings to their children.

## STRIKING INCIDENTS, AND BRIEF ACCOUNTS OF DISTINGUISHED MOTHERS.

I. ENCOURAGEMENT TO PRAYING MOTHERS.—William —— was the only surviving son of a pious mother. He was a boy of good parts, but of an unpromising and untoward disposition. This occasioned much anxiety to his mother, even in his childhood; and, as may be readily imagined, her anxiety increased with his growing years.

Having finished his education, he came to reside at home, and was soon after apprenticed to a respectable profession. Now the mother's trial became greater than ever. He paid little or no respect to her, and showed a particular aversion to everything like serious religion. The death of two sisters was fresh in his recollection, and yet he behaved most unkindly to the only one who survived. His conduct to his master and to his fellow-apprentices was equally unamiable, and even profane swearing was his frequent practice. At this time, his mother hardly ever durst address an admonition to him, prayer was almost her only hope and refuge. As one fault after another obtruded itself on her notice, she set apart additional seasons for special prayer on his behalf: till at length her strength and spirits were so exhausted with the continual excitement, that she almost felt as if she must give up

the effort.   She had already resigned four dear children into the arms of death, in the full assurance that
they had gone to be with Christ, which was far better
than remaining with their parents.   But this *one* occupied her last waking thoughts at night, and her first in
the morning ; and respecting him, she could truly say,
that she had "sorrow in her heart daily."   He still,
however, attended the preaching of the Gospel ; and
on one occasion sat by her side, while she listened with
inexpressible emotions to a sermon on the final judgment, in which her minister warned the impenitent,
that even their pious relations, who had wept and
prayed for them, would acquiesce in their condemnation.

With a heavy heart the mother returned home, and
as soon as she had taken off her bonnet, threw herself on her knees, and once more commended her beloved child to the mercy and grace of God.   She says,
"her prayer was more nearly allied to the expression
of despair, than the exercise of faith."   But she was
soon to experience that the Lord's thoughts were not
as her thoughts—

> "Just in the last distressing hour,
>     The Lord displays delivering power."

On coming out of her room, she was greeted by a
voice of unusual mildness, saying, "Mother, Mr.
M—— has preached the best sermon to-day that he
ever did in his life."   She replied, "Ah! William, it
is difficult to say which is a minister's best sermon ;

perhaps it is, that our ears have been opened to hear differently."

Nothing more passed at that time, but during the succeeding days, his behavior was kind and pleasant. On the Saturday evening, he said, " I think we have had a happy week, mother; I hope Mr. M—— will have another good sermon to-morrow." What he heard on that Sabbath, however, did not call forth any particular remark. But on the Sabbath following, a stranger preached, whose sermon was much blessed to William; and from that time he began to speak freely to his mother on spiritual things, and to manifest a spirit of constant inquiry. To use her own expression, " she now found a son, and her daughter found a brother." They were so happy together, that she thought it was too much for earth, and would not last. He was remarkable for his regular attention to the duties of the closet. Even when company were with them in an evening, he would retire for half an hour after tea, and on the very last morning that dawned on him in this world, his father having asked him to do something in the garden, he replied, " I must go up stairs for half an hour first, and then I will, fa-ther." He was received into the church with great satisfaction; and twice his mother had the delight of sitting down with him at the Lord's table. Many a mother looked at them with a wistful eye, and wished such a privilege; but two days after the second of these hallowed occasions, his spirit was sud-denly called to mingle in the worship of the upper

sanctuary.   He was not permitted to give a dying testimony of his faith, but his living evidence of a change
of heart had for two years been most satisfactory.   His
death unsealed the lips of many who had silently admired his character ; and his master in particular, who
had the best opportunities of judging, and who is not
a professor of religion, gave a most unequivocal testimony to the remarkable change in his conduct.   His
pastor was absent at the time he joined the church,
and longed to return that he might acknowledge him
a younger brother in the Lord, and direct his youthful
energies into channels of Christian activity.   But, as if
the joy of his restoration to his family and flock needed
something to qualify it, he found these pleasing anticipations disappointed.

This hasty sketch is intended, like his own brief history, to teach Christian mothers to " be patient in trib-
ulation, and instant in prayer."


II. REV. RICHARD HOOKER.—This eminent divine
was deeply indebted to the early teachings of a pious
mother.   He was distinguished from childhood for his
diligence, and the propriety of his conduct.   During
his youth he was dangerously ill—when his afflicted
mother ceased not earnestly to beg his life of God, as
Monica, the mother of Augustine did, that he might
become a true Christian.   Her prayers were answered,
which her son in after life would often mention with
great gratitude.   " And has often prayed that he might
never live to occasion any sorrow to so good a mother,

of whom he would often say he loved her so dearly, that he would endeavor to be good, even as much for hers as for his own sake."

III. Rev. Philip Henry.—This eminent servant of God was the son of a pious mother who "feared God above many." She looked well to the ways of her household, prayed with them daily, catechised her children, and taught them the knowledge of the Lord betimes. He often mentioned, with thankfulness to God, his great happiness in having such a mother, who was to him as Lois and Eunice were to Timothy, acquainting him with the Scriptures in his childhood. There appeared in him early inclinations both to learning and piety, so that his mother devoted him in his tender years to the service of God in the work of the ministry. This excellent mother died before her son was quite fourteen years old, but her influence over him remained throughout life, and was ever prompting him to be faithful unto death, that he might inherit the crown of everlasting life.

IV. Rev. John Bailey.—This useful minister of the Gospel in Ireland and New England, was born Feb. 25th, 1643, near Blackburn, in Lancashire. His pious mother dedicated him, even before he was born, to the service of God. "From a child, he knew the Holy Scriptures, and was by them made wise unto salvation, through faith which is in Christ Jesus." He gave evidence of his gracious state, by his habitual fear of God, and the practice of daily prayer. This was attended with one very remarkable and happy effect.

17

His father was a wicked man, and his mother took her son, while he was yet a child, and calling the family together, caused him to pray for them. His father, hearing how the child prayed with the family, was so struck with conviction, that it proved the beginning of his conversion to God. This pious youth, at the age of 22, entered on the work of the ministry at Chester, and continued, in the distant lands to which he was called, faithful unto the end.

V. REV. ANTHONY CROLE.—Anthony Crole was a native of Kincardineshire, Scotland. At the age of seven years he was left to the charge of a widowed mother, who took care that he should enjoy the privilege of a religious education. This excellent woman discharged the trust that devolved upon her with great faithfulness and ability. She watched for the souls of her children as one that must give an account. Her instruction and example made a lasting impression on Anthony's mind, and he would frequently mention the familiar way in which she would encourage her children to seek the God of their fathers, saying, "God loves to hear little children pray;" and from this early period prayer was never omitted by her son, who lived to be a useful and honored minister of the Gospel of Christ.

VI. REV. GEORGE BELL.—This pious and useful man was a native of North Britain. The risings of early depravity and folly were checked in him by the unwearied care and watchfulness of a mother possessing singular piety and prudence, and to the close of his life, he used to speak of his singular obligations to the training of his mother, who, though she died while he was yet young, had sown seed in his mind that subsequently brought forth abundantly.

VII. Rev. Dr. Samuel Annesley.—This distinguished man, who was the father of Mrs. Wesley, was born at Kenilworth, in 1620. He was an only child, and his father dying when he was only four years old, his education devolved on his pious mother, who was eminently qualified for the task, bringing him up in the nurture and admonition of the Lord. The effect of her training so decidedly turned his mind to serious things, that he formed the resolution, if God should spare him until he reached manhood, to devote himself to His service by preaching the everlasting Gospel. Though this resolve was made at a very early age, he never swerved from it, and proved the sincerity of his desire by becoming a very eminent and zealous servant of God.

VIII. Mrs. Lucy Hutchinson.—This justly celebrated woman, in her interesting biography of her admirable husband, says, after celebrating the land of her birth, " The next blessing I have to consider in my nativity is my parents, both of them pious instructors of my youth, both by precept and example; and it pleased God, by the teachings of my pious mother, and the sermons she carried me to, that I was convinced the knowledge of God was the most excellent study, and his service the most worthy employment of my life."

IX. REV. W. B. CADOGAN.—It was the privilege of this excellent minister to have, like Timothy, a mother and grandmother who were both piously disposed, and who instructed him from his infancy in the Holy Scriptures. And late in life, he bore testimony to the value of maternal instructions, by saying, " I am persuaded, from the impressions made by a pious mother on my own mind, when a child, that very few parents sufficiently *aim*, or sufficiently *hope* in their religious endeavors with their children."

X. REV. THOMAS UPPENDINE.—This holy and consistent servant of God was born at Wallsall, in Staffordshire, and was the seventh of a family of eleven children, most of whom died young. His father was prejudiced against religion; but his mother, on the contrary, was a most pious and amiable woman, possessing great strength of mind and good sense. She strove by all means to counteract the evil tendency of her husband's example, by bestowing great pains on the religious education of her children. She had her reward. Those of her children who were spared to her became pious members of society; and her son Thomas was from his youth distinguished for his seriousness, and lived to adorn the Gospel of his Saviour, by a useful life as a Christian minister, and a triumphant death.

XI. REV. JAMES DAVIS KNOWLES.—(Professor in the Baptist Theological Institution, Newton, Massachusetts.)—It was the peculiar privilege of this faithful minister to be the son of pious parents. He was born at Providence, in the United States, in 1798. At the age of twelve years, he was left by the death of his father to the future charge of his mother, who was qualified by her eminent piety to instruct and admonish him. Very early he began to display very great intellectual superiority, contributing to local periodicals at an early age. His mother, by her sympathy, encouraged his literary pursuits, and lived to see him become one of the most zealous and talented ministers of his time.

XII. Rev. James C. Crane. — Secretary of the United Foreign Missionary Society, was born in Morristown, United States, January 11th, 1794. The faithful instructions of his mother made a deep impression upon him at the tender age of six years. He was subsequently apprenticed in New York, where amidst temptations he fell into vicious habits; but in consequence of the lessons of his mother, he experienced such severe rebukes of conscience, that he was constrained to seek Divine mercy as a repentant sinner, and dedicated his life to the propagation of the Gospel as a missionary among the tribes of the North American Indians, in which work he became eminently distinguished.

XIV. Rev. Samuel Davies. — This distinguished man, who was President of Princeton College, New Jersey, was born November 3, 1724. He was an only son; a daughter had been born to his parents five years before his birth. His mother, an eminent Chris-

17*

tian, had earnestly besought him of heaven, and believing him to be given in answer to prayer, she named him Samuel.  This excellent woman took upon herself the task of teaching her son to read, as there was no school in the neighborhood, and her efforts were rewarded by the extraordinary proficiency of her pupil. In early life, his mind was not very deeply impressed with religious convictions; but at length the prayers of his pious mother were answered; he became savingly converted to Christ, and commenced laboring in the ministry at the age of 22.  Being an eminent scholar, and very active in his duties, his labors obtained him the evident blessing of God, and the approbation of man.  Few men did more in their day and generation to promote the extension of the Saviour's kingdom in the world.

XV.  Thomas Pringle, Esq.—This eminent philanthropist, whose name deserves to be held in veneration as a benefactor of the human race, was born at Blaiklau, Roxburghshire, January 5, 1789.  His childhood was passed amid the pastoral and secluded scenery of a farm-house.   An accident in infancy caused him to be afflicted with lameness, which continued for life. The watchful care of a wise and judicious mother was exerted to prevent his being spoiled by the over indulgence of his nurse, who, compassionating his misfortune, was ignorantly adding to it by trying to spoil his temper by excessive indulgence.   It was his unspeakable misfortune to lose his faithful mother at the

early age of six years, but he retained a vivid remembrance of her to the end of his life. In a letter written many years after to a friend, he thus expresses
himself: "I recollect my mother distinctly, and particularly all the circumstances connected with the last
days of her life. How can I ever forget the last kind
and solemn words, the farewell smile, the parting embrace of my mother—of such a mother?" Doubtless
it was in answer to the prayers and dying faith of this
devoted woman that her son became the honored instrument of so much good to his fellow-creatures in
Scotland, South Africa, and in England; and that
the cause of the slave was ever near his heart, and
that his whole life exhibited a pattern of love to God
and love to man.

XVI. Rev. Luke Foster.—This faithful minister
of the Gospel was born at Glauton, Northumberland,
on the 25th May, 1801. His mother died while he
was yet a youth; but her lessons in his childhood, her
valuable instructions in life, and her solemn counsels
in death, were indelibly impressed on his heart, and
were among the principal means of his subsequent
conversion to God. Blackburn and Saffron Walden
were successively the scenes of his ministerial labors.
His life and death were alike honorable to the religion
that he taught.

XVII. Rev. Dr. Nevin's Mother.—His mother,
whose maiden name was Mary Hubbard, was an estimable woman, and very attentive to the religious

instruction of her children, teaching them, besides other things, that excellent summary of Christian doctrine, the Westminster Assembly's Catechism. The benefits of this instruction were with thankfulness acknowledged by her youngest son, during all his public life. This lady died in the year 1820. Twelve years after her death, he says, "The year 1820 is mournful in the retrospect. Our dear mother left us that year. But it was according to the course of nature that our mother should go before us to eternity, and she sank to the grave by a gradual decline, and full of years, having served her generation by the will of God."

XVIII. Rev. Richard Knill's Mother.—I have a vivid recollection of the effect of maternal influence. My honored mother was a religious woman, and she watched over and instructed me, as pious mothers are accustomed to do. Alas! I often forgot her admonitions; but in my most thoughtless days, I never lost the impressions which her holy example had made on my mind.

After spending a large portion of my life in foreign lands, I returned again to visit my native village. Both my parents died while I was in Russia, and their house is now occupied by my brother. The furniture remains just the same as when I was a boy; and at night I was accommodated with the same bed in which I had often slept before; but my busy thoughts would not let me sleep—I was thinking how God had led me through the journey of life. At last, the light of the morning darted through the little window, and then my eye caught a sight of the spot where my sainted mother, forty years before, took me by the hand and said, "Come, my dear, kneel down with me, and I will go to prayer."

This completely overcame me :—I seemed to hear the very tones of her voice—I recollected some of her expressions, and I burst into tears, and arose from my bed, and fell upon my knees, just on the spot where my mother kneeled, and thanked God that I had once a praying mother. And, oh! if every parent could feel what I felt then, I am sure they would pray WITH their children, as well as pray FOR them.

Chiratian mothers! think of this, and then think of the millions of your own sex who are the mere slaves of men who never pray. Remember, it is only where the Lord Jesus Christ is known and loved, that women are exalted to their proper place in society; and remember, also, it is only Christian missionaries and their wives, and a few teachers of schools, who have attempted to raise them. They have attempted it, and God has smiled upon their undertaking. But they need help—let them have it.

XIX. ANDREW JACKSON AND HIS MOTHER.—The deceased Ex-President had no half-way character. "He was known and read of all. He was a man to secure ardent friends and bitter enemies. He could disguise nothing. Simulation was a thing he abhorred as much by the instinct of his nature, as by the decision of his judgment.

In a conversation with the writer of this article, some years since, Gen. J. spoke of his mother in a manner that convinced me, that his mother never ceased to exert a secret power over him, until his heart was brought into reconciliation with God. She had three sons, Hugh, Robert, and Andrew, the youngest, whose father died not long after his birth, little prescient of the future fame of his poor boy, whom his mother, with the scanty patrimony, could scarcely educate. But he said that she inculcated religious truth upon his mind. The leading doctrines of the Bible were taught him in the form of question and answer, as contained in the Westminster Catechism. In those truths, he expressed his decided belief. But their saving power does not seem to have been felt for more than half a century afterward. I think he was about seventy when he united with the church. Few of his friends will probably claim for him the possession of piety while he was the occupant of the Presidential chair, however much in such a perilous position its sovereign virtue is needed to guide the judgment, repress the ambition, chasten the language, and subdue the passions of the conspicuous incumbent of that coveted seat. In retirement, it was different; there he could reflect more deeply, feel more tenderly, and choose more deliberately. One can hardly help contrasting the cold and heartless sneers of Jefferson at the religion of Christ, with the full, warm, and enthusiastic expressions of Jackson, in the all-sufficient merits of the atoning Redeemer."

The old man was characteristic to the last. Whatever he resolved to do, he was never ashamed of. Of the Bible, he said—"Upon that sacred volume I rest my hope for eternal salvation, through the merits and the blood of our blessed Lord and Saviour, Jesus Christ." Let all his admirers mark this. Not alone in his unbelief did Jefferson live and die. He drew after him many that, in the blindness of their delusion, looked to him as well for a creed in religion as in politics. Will the example and influence of Jackson be equally strong on the belief of the devoted admirers, who are charmed with his military and civic qualities ?

XX. RANDOLPH'S MOTHER.—The mother of John Randolph taught his infant lips to pray. This fact he never could forget. It influenced his whole life, and saved him from the dangers of infidelity. He was one day speaking on the subject of infidelity, to which he had been exposed by his intercourse with men of infidel principles, to a distinguished Southern gentleman, and used this remarkable language :—

"I believe I should have been swept away by the flood of French infidelity, if it had not been for one thing—the remembrance of the time when my sainted mother used to make me kneel by her side, taking my little hands folded in hers, and cause me to repeat the Lord's Prayer."

Every mother who reads this anecdote, may read an important practical lesson, which she ought to put to use in the case of her own children. No mother can ever know how great and salutary will be the influence on her little son, on all his future life in this world, and in the world to come, of teaching him to pray. How appropriate, how beautiful the conduct of that mother, who teaches her little son to kneel by her side as he retires to rest, to lift up his young heart to the God that made him, and on whose care and mercy he must rely in all the future years of his existence! If all mothers would teach their children to pray, and pray with and for them, how soon would this world's aspect be changed, and bud and blossom as the rose! And the mother who does not teach her children to pray, has no good ground to believe that she shall ever meet her children in heaven, or that she will ever reach there herself. Prayerless mothers never find admittance to heaven.

XXI. THE MOTHER OF THE REV. GEORGE BEECHER. —The humble, weary, and anxious toils of the nursery sometimes need glimpses of the future, to impart to them their true dignity and value. Let any mother who feels that she is of small value, and that her duties and cares are of little account, ponder over such incidents as these.

On the east end of Long Island, in one of the most secluded spots in this country (America), more than thirty years ago, a mother, whose rare intellectual and moral endowments were known to but few, made this simple record:

" This morning I rose very early to pray for my children; and especially that my sons may be ministers and missionaries of Jesus Christ."

A number of years after, a friend who was present,

thus describes this mother's dying hour: "Owing to extreme weakness, her mind wandered, and her conversation was broken; but as she entered the valley of the shadow of death, her soul lighted up and gilded its darkness. She made a feeling and most appropriate prayer, and told her husband that her views and anticipations had been such, that she could scarcely sustain them; and that if they had been increased, she should have been overwhelmed; that her Saviour had blessed her with constant peace, and that through all her sickness, she had never prayed for life. She dedicated her five sons to God as ministers and missionaries of Jesus Christ, and said that her greatest desire was, that her children might be trained up for God.

"She spoke with joy of the advancement of the kingdom of Christ, and of the glorious day now ushering in. She attempted to speak to her children, but was so exhausted, and their cries and sobs were such, that she could say but little. Her husband then made a prayer, in which he gave her back to God, and dedicated all they held in common to him. She then fell into a sweet sleep, from which she awoke in heaven."

The prayers of this mother have been answered. All her eight children have been "trained up for God." Her five sons are all "ministers and missionaries of Jesus Christ." And the late Rev. George Beecher is the first of her offspring whom she has welcomed to heaven.

18

XXII. A Wise Mother.—The mother of a family was married to an infidel who made a jest of religion in the presence of his own children; yet she succeeded in bringing them all up in the fear of the Lord. I one day asked her how she had preserved them from the influence of a father whose sentiments were so openly opposed to her own. This was her answer: "Because to the authority of a father I did not oppose the authority of a mother, but that of God. From their earliest years my children have always seen the Bible upon my table. This holy book has constituted the whole of their religious instruction. I was silent that I might allow it to speak. Did they propose a question? Did they commit any fault? Did they perform any good action? I opened the Bible, and the Bible answered, reproved, or encouraged them. The constant reading of the Scriptures has alone wrought the prodigy which surprises you."

XXIII. A Mother's Prayers.—In a seaport town of New England lived a pious mother of six daughters. At the age of sixty, she had been for many years subject to disease and infirmity, which confined her to her house, and almost to her room. In an interview one day with a friend, she said—"I had not for many years enjoyed the pleasure of going to the house of God with his people, and taking sweet counsel with them. But I have another source of grief greater than this—one that weighs down my spirits day and night! while disease and pain bear my body toward the grave." Her friend tenderly inquired the cause of this peculiar grief. She replied, " I have six daughters; two are married and live near me, and four are with me; but not one of them gives any evidence of piety. I am alone. I have no one for a Christian companion. O that even one of them were pious, that I might walk alone no longer." Such was her language. Yet she seemed submissive to the will of God, whatever it might be, having strong confidence, that in his own good time, he would answer her daily prayers, and in a way which would best advance his glory.

Not long after the above interview, a revival of religion commenced in the town in which she lived. Among the first subjects of this work were four of her daughters. A fifth was soon added to their number, but the other, the eldest, remained unmoved. One day one of the young converts proposed to her mother and her converted sisters to observe a day of fasting and prayer for the sister who remained so insensible. The agreement was made, and a day observed. Of this the subject of their prayers had no knowledge. But on the same day, while engaged in her domestic concerns at home, her mind was solemnly arrested; and she was soon added to the Christian sisterhood.

The praying mother lived a few years to enjoy their Christian society. They surrounded her dying bed, received her last blessing, and unitedly commended her spirit to God.

XXIV. The Power of a Mother.—A youth who had been piously educated, had long grieved his parents by his misconduct. Reproof, expostulation, correction, had been repeatedly tried without success; and he had arrived at an age when parents can no longer exercise absolute control. He left home under circumstances truly distressing to his parents; but which seemed to produce no effect upon his mind. Not long afterward, he received a parcel from home. As he examined its various contents, and found one proof after another of a mother's tender, considerate care for the health and comfort of one so undeserving; and found, too, a letter fraught with kindness and affection, and without one word of upbraiding, the rebel's heart melted within him. He fell on his knees and blessed God for giving him such a mother—wept bitterly over his own ingratitude and disobedience—implored pardon through the blood of atonement, and sought the strength of Divine grace to enable him to be *their* comfort whose grief he had long been. The expressions of genuine penitence that accompanied his acknowledgment of that communication, led the parents to give utterance to their feelings of joy and gratitude in the language of the Jews of old:—"The Lord hath done great things for us; whereof we are glad. They that sow in tears shall reap in joy." Christian mothers, amidst all your trials, cherish the like encouragements; for still the word is on record and in force: "He that goeth forth weeping, bearing precious seed, shall doubtless come again with rejoicing, bringing his sheaves with him."—Psa. cxxvi.

## MOTHER, HOME AND HEAVEN.

" The sounds that fall on mortal ear,
   As dew drops pure at even,
That soothe the breast, or start the tear,
   Are mother, home, and heaven.

A mother—sweetest name on earth !
   We lisp it on the knee,
And idolize its sacred worth
   In manhood's infancy.

A home—that paradise below,
   Of sunshine and of flowers,
Where hallowed joys perennial flow,
   By calm sequestered bowers.

And heaven—the port of endless peace,
   The haven of the soul,
When life's corroding care shall cease,
   Like sweeping waves to roll.

O weep not, then, though cruel time
   The chain of love has riven ;
To every link, in yonder clime,
   Reunion shall be given.

O fall they not on mortal ear
   As dew drops pure at even,
To soothe the breast or start the tear—
   A mother, home, and heaven ?"

XXV. A Remembrance of a Mother's Influence.
—What a mercy to be early inducted into the kingdom
of grace ! How happy are they who choose Christ for
their portion while young, and devote to God the first
fruits of their lives ! How good to grow up into Chrst
our living head, and to hold fast the beginning of our
confidence steadfast to the end !. How pleasant to take
a retrospect of such a life, and how blessed the pros-

18*

pect which opens to the view of all such! Would that the young would wisely consider, and make the happy choice.

"I must, at least, advert to the instrumentalities which it pleased God to employ, by which to bring me to himself. I am a child of many prayers. I was blest with a pious mother, who had learned to pray before I was born; a duty which she loved and practiced to the end of her life. The recollections of that mother—that devout and praying mother—awaken a reminiscence of the past, which now warms my poor heart, and touches the tenderest chords that vibrate to my sympathies. Mother! What name on earth that is so fraught with everything that is touching, tender, and endearing? What multitudes of events cluster around that name, which act upon the finer feelings of the soul and soften the asperity of the human heart! Mother! is a word that has made the iron heart of the most unfeeling and cruel yield, and brought back the sympathies of childhood, and annihilated, for the time, the hardening influence of those rugged scenes of life through which men, in the more mature periods of their earthly existence, often pass. 'Rome is saved, but your son is lost,' was once the language of a son moved by the maternal influence of a mother's presence and a mother's tears.

"The thoughts of a mother's prayers, and the recollections of her many pious admonitions, often checked me in my wildest career of sin, though she knew it not. I concealed my feelings from her. I often felt the deepest when I put on the appearance of the greatest gayety. And I have often wondered that her patience did not become worn out with me. But no—hers was a mother's love! At length I yielded, and hastened home to tell her what God had done for my poor soul. It was a meeting that even poetry would fail to describe. She wept and rejoiced over me. We bowed around the family altar together, and poured out our souls in prayer and praise. O, it was a scene that angels must have rejoiced over.

Mothers, be faithful. Don't get discouraged. Pray for your children, and do not forget to talk to them: your words will settle down in their hearts. They never can, they never will forget them. They may appear not to heed what you say; they may put on an appearance of thoughtlessness and levity, which look as though your words were disregarded; but persevere—those words are there, and never will be forgotten: but may be called up in years to come when you are dead and gone, and like seed cast in the earth, germinate and produce fruit that shall flourish in immortality.

"My own dear mother is dead; but, though dead, yet she speaks. She lived, however, to see the fruit of her labors, and so may you. My mother lived to hear me preach the Gospel. The parting scene I shall never forget, when I bade her adieu to go out into the vineyard of my Lord. 'I always hoped,' said she, 'to have you home with me, to comfort and support me in my declining years, but the Lord has called, and I must submit. Go, my son, and be faithful, and the

Lord be with thee and bless thee,' and she turned her face to the wall and wept.

"A few days before she departed, she had an impression that she would soon finish her course. She went to the door and called my father, and as he came into the house, she burst into a flood of tears, and said, 'I shall never see my son S—— again.' My sister was called, and a charge given to her—'I am going in a few days,' was her language, 'and I wish you to make arrangements for my funeral. My grave-clothes are in such a drawer," &c. In about twenty-four hours she was taken with a chill. 'This is the messenger' said she, and in three days she closed her eyes in death, in great peace. Her last words were, 'Tell all my children to meet me in heaven!'

> "My mother! when I learned that thou wast dead,
> Say, wast thou conscious of the tears I shed?
> Hover'd thy spirit o'er thy sorrowing son?"

XXVII. A FACT FOR MOTHERS.—The following fact, which the writer obtained from a member of the family to which it belongs, and who is a worthy minister of the Gospel, strikingly illustrates and confirms the declaration of God to Eli, "Them that honor me, I will honor." The matron who is the heroine of this short but interesting story was neither wealthy nor learned; but she was one that feared God with all her house, bringing up her children in the nurture and admonition of the Lord. And as she honored God, so God honored her with long life, and numerous descendants.

In the district of Beaufort, South Carolina, U. S., one of the most affecting scenes was witnessed that probably ever occurred. The lady in question, at the age of seventy-six, determined once more to enjoy the society of all her children and grandchildren then living, and accordingly requested them to spend a day with her. The interview was most affecting, and was conducted just as we should suppose piety and the relation sustained by the parties would dictate. She acknowledged God in this, as well as in every other way. Her eldest son, who is a minister of the Gospel in the Baptist denomination, commenced the exercises of the day, by reading the Scriptures and prayer. The whole family then joined in a song of praise to the Giver of every good and perfect gift. This service was concluded by a suitable exhortation from the same person. Eighty-five of her regular descendants were present. Forty-four children and grandchildren, arrived at maturity, sat at the same table at dinner. Of that number, forty-three professed faith in Jesus Christ; of the four surviving sons of this excellent lady, two were preachers of the Gospel, and the other two deacons in the Baptist church.

Two of her grandsons were also ministers of the same church. When the day was drawing to a close, the matron called her numerous children around her, gave them each salutary advice and counsel, and bestowed upon all her parting blessing. The day was closed by her youngest son, with exercises similar to those with which it commenced.

Mrs. —— lived eight years after this event, leaving, at her death, one hundred and fifteen lineal descendants, in which large number not a swearer nor drunkard is to be found.

Now who can estimate all the blessings which will accrue to the human family, from the piety and prudence of this one family?

What may we not hope from the four ministers?

XXIX. REV. DR. WAUGH AND HIS MOTHER.—Few names of modern times will be more affectionately and gratefully remembered than that of Dr. Waugh, the respected minister of the Secession Church, Wells street, one of the founders of the London Missionary Society, and a man whose influence and labors, for more than forty years, were devoted to all the great and benevolent institutions of his day. It is evident that the formation of his character is distinctly traceable to maternal influence.

Concerning his mother, Dr. Waugh has left the following account:—" Piety and meekness, and the tenderest regard for the happiness of her children, formed the outline of her character. Born of eminently pious parents, Alexander Johnstone, farmer in East Gordon, and Elizabeth Waugh, her mind at an early period was formed to the love of goodness. Through life she maintained the character of a godly, modest, and inoffensive woman. Her devotions were regular and fervent: the law of kindness to all was on her lips; but toward her children her affection was uncommonly strong, and her religious principles directed her affection into the path of tender solicitude about their eternal welfare. By prayer, by exhortation, by example, and by many tears, did she study to advance our knowledge of the true God, and Jesus Christ whom he hath sent. She had herself experienced the sweetness of unaffected godliness, and was greatly concerned that her children might also taste and see that the Lord is gracious."

"Few men have attained to high eminence, either in science or religion, who have not expressed deep-felt gratitude for the example, and counsels, and prayers of an affectionate and pious mother; and in the case of Dr. Waugh, this grateful feeling was strikingly manifested. It were injustice to her memory not to record most prominently the reverential affection with which he ever spoke of the character of his mother. It was his delight to breathe into the ears of his own children the story of her piety and kindness; to her he looked back, even at the age of threescore years and ten, with all the humility and fondness of a child; and when, nearly forty years after her death, he heard the summons issued that was to gather him to his fathers, his filial tenderness, as will be seen at the closing account of his life, even then prompted the wish, that his pillow could have been softened by the hand of his mother, and his heart refreshed and strengthened by her prayers!—thus recommending on his death-bed the performance of that duty to which he was ever so anxious to direct the attention of the young,—'Honor thy father and thy mother.'

"The laudable exertions of this excellent parent in the religious education of her children, were followed by a rich recompense of reward. With a mind constituted like hers, she tasted the sweetest of all pleasures, in beholding her three children give satisfactory evidence of fearing God from their youth."

## XXX. THE ABSENT MOTHER.

### BY MRS. E. H. EVANS.

My mother's name ! it hath the power
To cheer, at once, my saddest hour ;
The vision of my mother's form
Methinks might quell grief's wildest storm.

It will be endless joy to me,
If I again that form shall see—
Sorrow and pain shall both be o'er,
If I regain her side once more.

I was a little, thoughtless child,
When last she looked on me and smiled,
And when they took me from her side,
My April tears by sleep were dried.

Others may wander far away
From homes a mother's smiles make gay,
And sicken with the yearnings vain,
To look upon her face again ;

Yet if, perchance, they meet once more,
The freshness of their youth is o'er,
And she their love hath pined to see,
Is passing from the household tree.

Or, if not thus, harsh thoughts will rise
To loosen e'en the holiest ties ;
A random word on either part,
May fill with grief the loving heart.

But oh, my mother, when we meet,
Say what can mar our union sweet?
What cloud shall darken in the eyes
That gaze abroad on Paradise?

No grief-traced lines on either face
Shall sadden in that first embrace;
But, beaming both with love's own light,
Shall make the air around us bright.

Mother, there is another form
Escaped from life and sorrow's storm;
'Tis she who gave the loved one birth,
Now dearest to thy child on earth.

I love her memory for his sake,
And often when the stars awake
I sit in silence by his side,
To hear how, like a saint, she died!

Say, are ye sisters in one band?
Perchance, e'en side by side ye stand!
With rays of equal glory crowned;
Harps of the same melodious sound.

Yet could I look upon ye so,
Methinks, at once, my heart would know
Which was the dearest one to me,
The watcher of my infancy.

'Tis all a fancy—yet I deem,
Thine eyes would more intensely beam,
Thy lip would wear a lovelier smile,
Gazing upon thy child the while.

A mother's love would light thy face,
And lend thy form a softer grace;
Thy voice have cadence more divine—
Nay, e'en thy robes more brightly shine.

Sweet spirit! shall it ever be
That I may dwell again with thee?
O, Death shall wear an angel's charms,
If he conduct me to thine arms!

19

## XXXI. TO A BEREAVED MOTHER.

### ON THE DEATH OF A LITTLE CHILD.

NOT long ago I saw thee,
  And joy was in thy tread;
Bounding along so free,
Thy little friend by thee,
  But now thou'rt with the dead.

Fond words were spoken then,
  Fond looks were cast on thee;
But now thou art at rest,
Not on thy mother's breast,
  Not on thy father's knee.

Young dweller of the sky,
  Thy home is far above;
Now in thy Shepherd's arms,
Thou'rt safe from all alarms,
  Safe with the source of love.

Thy mother weeps for thee;
  The Saviour says she may;
But if thou couldst impart
Some word to cheer her heart,
  What wouldst thou say?

Oh! it is well with me, mother!
  In the uncorrupted land,
Where hang the fadeless leaves,
From the nation's healing trees
  See thy little Bessie stand.

Mother! 'tis well with me;
  When waking on thy bed,
When musing thoughts by day,
That will not pass away,
  Remember—I'm not dead.

Mother! 'tis well with me;
  For though my body lie

Down in a grassy nest,
The part thou didst love best
    Can never—never die.

Mother! 'tis well with me;
    I join the angel band;
I praise my Shepherd-king
In strains I could not sing,
    Down in your mortal land.

Mother! 'tis well with me,
    Thy lamb untask'd—untried—
The fight was fought for me,
I've won the victory,
    And I will welcome thee
        Among the sanctified.

                    British Mother's Magazine.


XXXII. THE GRANDMOTHER'S DEATH.—AS I was
sitting, says an American writer, at my door, one of
the unusually lovely evenings with which we have
been favored this spring, watching the playfulness of
my two little children, who were running through the
walks of the garden, and now and then stopping to
gather a sweet-scented purple, or white violet, with
which the whole air was perfumed, I saw at a little
distance the carriage of a dear and intimate friend,
which quickly drove to the door, and my friend alight-
ed. I noticed nothing peculiar in his demeanor, until he
drew my little girl toward him, and with a solemn
manner, said, "Lizzie, your grandmother is dead; you
will never see her." "Dead!" I exclaimed; "have
you a letter?" "Yes;" and, as he turned to hand
me the letter, I saw the look of utter despondency,
and *felt* that he *had* lost a *mother*.

That mother and that son were equally devoted to each other. He was the youngest of six children. They had been for years separated, and he had bright anticipations of seeing her in a few short weeks, and presenting his two little cherished ones whom she had so often heard of, but never seen. Alas! alas! these anticipations are all blighted now; and, Lizzie, your dear grandmother is dead; you will never see her, still rings in my ears as when I first heard it.

But the aged mother was a Christian; and the letter says, "her reason was clear during her whole sickness; not a murmur did she utter, but was *anxious to depart.*" And, doubtless, long ere this, she has beheld "the King in his beauty," and been introduced to scenes of glory, where even the cherubim, so long accustomed to celestial visions, veil their faces. What now to her seems the pilgrimage of threescore years and ten? She has entered eternity. What to her the sorrows and afflictions which once grieved her? "Not worthy to be compared with the glory *now* revealed." With holy rapture, she bows before the throne, and adores the Trinity. I think I see her, not as once I saw her, clothed in sable robes, and mourning that death had entered her household. No; death has at last proved her friend, separated the mortal from the immortal, and ushered her into the felicities of heaven. There, clothed in a white robe, with a crown upon her brow, a harp in her hand, unfading youth in her countenance, and the fullness of joy in her heart, she looks to the completion of time upon earth, as the perfection of her existence, in eternity, in heaven. Then, at the sound of the Archangel's trumpet, that friend which so long had enshrined her spirit, and been the servant of her will, that *body*, purified, ennobled, immortalized, will rush once more to her companionship, and they two, being one, shall " dwell forever with the Lord."

The resurrection of the body, the immortality of the soul, the divinity, the atonement, the intercession of Christ, the perpetuity of happiness—what elevating—what glorious doctrines are these! A wonderful destiny is ours ;—entering the world the most helpless of all earthly beings, progressing, step by step, until we become but " little lower than the angels," reaching an elevation superior to that of any created intelligence.

Does that sainted mother now regret having given her lifetime to her Maker? Does she wish she had lived the life of the moralist, and enjoyed *some* of the pleasures of *sin* for a *season?* If a blush of shame can burn upon the countenances of the inhabitants of heaven, it is when they think of the inexhaustible love of God toward them, and their unaccountable ingratitude.

The lamp of the moralist may serve to light his steps as far as a sick-bed, but we may rest assured, so soon as death appears, even in the distance, its flame will weaken and then expire; there will be naught to direct his path through the " dark valley and the shadow of death," but the lightnings of Divine wrath, the glarings of the lake that burneth.

19*

The Christian's pathway through the dark valley is first cheered by the dawnings of the Sun of Righteousness; the further he advances, the plainer becomes the passage, and the more dazzling the brilliancy, until at length he enters heaven, where there is "no need of the sun; for the glory of God doth lighten it."

XXXIII. The Mother in the Closet. — Some years since, a fine young man, the only son of his mother, and she a widow, on becoming of age and receiving his patrimony, entered into company, and indulged in the dissipation of genteel society. Her watchful eye saw his danger, pointed out its tendency to ruin body and soul, and used every argument, persuasion, and entreaty in vain. One day, she learned he was to dine with a large and joyful party, and she spent the forenoon in persuading him to relinquish it, but all in vain. "Mother, I will go!" "Then, John, I will retire to my closet, and pray for you till I see your face again." He went to the party, but could find no enjoyment; the thought of his mother, being on her knees wrestling with God in prayer for him, formed such a contrast to the scene before him, that he slipped away—found his mother in the act of prayer—knelt down by her—fell on her neck—and from that day became the delight of his pious mother—a brand plucked from the burning! A religious parent's prayers are seldom offered in vain.

## XXXIV. BIRTH-DAY VERSES—TO MY MOTHER.

### BY N. P. WILLIS.

My birth-day!  Oh, beloved mother!
  My heart is with thee o'er the seas!
I did not think to count another
  Before I wept upon thy knees—
Before this scroll of absent years
Was blotted with thy streaming tears.

My own I do not care to check—
  I weep—albeit here alone—
As if I hung upon thy neck,
  As if thy lips were on my own—
As if this full, sad heart of mine
Were beating closely upon thine.

Four weary years! how looks she now?
  What light is in those tender eyes?
What trace of time has touched the brow
  Whose look is borrowed of the skies
That listen to her nightly prayer?
How is she changed, since *he* was there
  Who sleeps upon her heart alway—
Whose name upon her lip is worn,
  For whom the night seems made to pray—
For whom she wakes to pray at morn,
Whose sight is dim—whose heart-strings stir—
Who weeps those tears—to think of *her!*

I know not if my mother's eyes
  Would find me changed in other things:
I've wandered beneath many skies,
  And tasted many bitter springs,
And many leaves, once fair and gay,
From youth's full flower have dropped away—
  But as these looser leaves depart,
The lessen'd flower gets near the core,
  And when deserted quite, the heart
Takes closer what was dear of yore,
And leans to those who loved it first—
The sunshine and the dew by which its bud was nursed

Dear mother ! dost thou love me yet ?
　Am I remembered in my home ?
When those I love for joy are met,
　Does some one wish that I would come ?
Thou *dost !* I *am* beloved of thee—
　But as the schoolboy numbers o'er
Night after night the Pleiades,
　And finds the stars he found before ;
As turns the maiden oft her token,
　As counts the miser oft his gold,
So, 'till life's " silver cord is broken,"
　Would I of thy dear love be told—
My heart is full—mine eyes are wet—
Dear mother ! dost thou love thy long-lost wanderer yet ?

Oh ! when the hour to meet again
　Creeps on—and, speeding o'er the sea,
My heart takes up its lengthen'd chain,
　And, link by link, draws nearer thee—
When land is hailed, and from the shore
　Comes off the blessed breath of home,
With fragrance from my mother's door
　Of flowers forgotten when I come—
When port is gained, and, slowly now,
　The old familiar paths are past,
And entering, unconscious how,
　I gaze upon thy face at last,
And run to thee, all faint and weak—
And feel thy tears upon my cheek—
　Oh ! if my heart break not with joy,
The light of heaven will fairer seem,
　And I shall grow once more a boy,
And ! mother !—'t will be like a dream
　That we were parted thus for years.
　And, once that we have dried our tears,
How will the days seem long and bright,
　To meet thee always with the morn,
And hear thy blessing every night—
　Thy " dearest," thy " first-born"—
And be no more, as now, in a strange land forlorn !

## XXXV. THE BLIND GIRL TO HER MOTHER.

"MOTHER, they say the stars are bright,
 And the broad heavens are blue—
I dream of them by day and night,
 And think them all like you.

I cannot touch the distant skies,
 The stars ne'er speak to me—
Yet their sweet images arise,
 And blend with thoughts of thee.

I know not why, but oft I dream
 Of the far land of bliss;
And when I hear thy voice, I deem
 That heaven is like to this.

When my sad heart to thine is pressed,
 My follies are forgiven,
Sweet pleasure warms my beating breast,
 And this I say is heaven.

O, mother, will the God above
 Forgive my faults like thee?
Will he bestow such care and love
 On a blind thing like me?

Dear mother, leave me not alone!
 Go with me when I die—
Lead thy blind daughter to the throne,
 And stay in yonder sky."

## XXXVI. I MISS THEE, MY MOTHER.

"I MISS thee, my mother! Thy image is still
 The deepest impressed on my heart,
And the tablet so faithful in death must be chill
 Ere a line of that image depart.
Thou wert torn from my side when I treasured thee most,
 When my reason could measure thy worth;
When I knew but too well that the idol I'd lost
 Could be never replaced upon earth.

I miss thee, my mother, in circles of joy,
    Where I've mingled with rapturous zest;
For how slight is the touch that will serve to destroy
    All the fairy web spun in my breast!
Some melody sweet may be floating around—
    'Tis a ballad I learnt at thy knee;
Some strain may be played, and I shrink from the sound,
    `For my fingers oft wake it for thee.

I miss thee, my mother; when young health has fled,
    And I sink in the languor of pain,
Where, where is the arm that once pillowed my head,
    And the ear that once heard me complain?
Other hands may support, gentle accents may fall—
    For the fond and the true are yet mine;
I've a blessing for each; I am grateful to all—
    But whose care *can* be soothing as thine?

I miss thee, my mother; in summer's fair day,
    When I rest in the ivy-wreath bower,
When I hang thy pet linnet's cage high on the spray,
    Or gaze on thy favorite flower.
There's the brightest gravel-path where I played by thy side,
    When time had scarce wrinkled thy brow,
Where I carefully led thee with worshiping pride,
    When thy scanty locks gathered the snow.

I miss thee, my mother! Oh, when do I not?
    Though I know 'twas the wisdom of Heaven
That the deepest shade fell on my sunniest spot,
    And such tie of devotion was riven;
For when thou wert with me my soul was below,
    I was chained to the world I then trod;
My affections, my thoughts, were all earth-bound; but now
    They have followed thy spirit to God!"

## XXXVII. LINES,

### BY THE REV. JOHN MARTIN, D.D.,

#### ON THE DEATH OF HIS MOTHER.

WEEP, weep, let all our kindred weep,
    Our parent gone, our pattern fled,
The object of our care to keep,
    Of love and duty, cold and dead!

Yet what is dead ?  'Tis but the dust,
  The vehicle, the tent, the shell ;
She as a burden, from her thrust,
  When soar'd her soul with Christ to dwell :—

To dwell, where long her wish had been,
  To know the bliss perfection gives,
To see Him, whom she loved unseen,
  Who for her died, and ever lives ;

And as she listens to the voice,
  Which comforts earth, and gladdens heaven,
Feel how celestials can rejoice,
  While thanks and praise to Him are given.

Count o'er the weeks, and days, and hours,
  Since she has enter'd Jesus' joy,
And would a selfish wish of yours
  Have kept her here from such employ ?

Would you those blissful moments still
  Had coursed beneath the cruel sway
Of anguish, baffling all our skill,
  Of longings, brooking ill delay ?

Count o'er, again, the golden days
  The saint has pass'd in yonder world,
And as you count, for each give praise,
  And be thy banner, Hope, unfurl'd—

The ecstatic hope, to join her there,
  To learn its wonders from her mouth,
In heaven's infancy her care,
  As we have been in earthly youth ;

To sing with her the hymns sublime,
  By angels fram'd, to Jesus' name ;
To learn her harp's harmonious chime,
  Like her, to celebrate His fame.

From where the parent shines on high,
  Oh, God ! the offspring shut not out ;
Guide us, Jehovah, with thine eye,
  And let thine angels camp about.

Purge us from vanity and pride,
  Low-thoughted sense, and selfish aims,

To live to Him, for us who died,
　　To feel and yield Him all his claims.

Protect us, by thy watchful power,
　　Through all the evils of our state ;
Like her, receive us at the hour
　　When death to heaven shall ope the gate.

### XXXVIII.  THE MOTHER'S GRAVE.

Lines suggested by the meeting of several members of the same family at the grave of their mother, after a separation of many years.

We parted when our young, glad hearts
　　From anxious care were free ;
We parted when the gay, green leaves
　　Were fresh on every tree ;
When youthful visions, bright and fair,
　　Came floating o'er the mind,
As shining clouds or fragrant air
　　Are borne upon the wind.

We parted when the summer birds
　　Warbled on every bough ;
And gurgling brooks, in leafy dells,
　　Made music, soft and low.
All bright and beautiful, the flowers
　　Their perfumes sweetly shed,—
Whence are you gone, ye happy hours ?
　　Alas ! ye all have fled.

We met again, when anxious care
　　Was seated on each brow,
And time had deeply written there
　　The marks of grief and woe.
No longer waved the branches green,
　　The flowers no perfume shed,
But wintry winds blew cold and keen
　　Across the violet's bed.

We met—but Oh ! what words can tell
　　The deep despair and gloom—
The choking sighs—the knees which fell
　　In sadness on the tomb
Of her who bless'd our infancy
　　With fond, maternal love ?—
We parted in despondency,—
　　*But hope to meet* ABOVE.

# SELECT ESSAYS

## ON

## MATERNAL DUTIES AND INFLUENCE.

---

### THE DIGNITY OF MOTHERS.

"MOTHER!" The name which is associated in every virtuous mind with all that is amiable and delightful. "Mother!" Most tender, endearing, and expressive of all human appellations! A title employed equally by the royal prince, the sage philosopher, and the untutored peasant,—by the savage and the civilized in all nations, and through all generations. A relation mercifully founded in the constitution of our nature—universally felt, and uniformly acknowledged. And who among all the children of men, except those who in early infancy were bereaved of their anxious parents, has not happily experienced the inexpressible influence of its charming and delightful power; who, of all the great and the mighty upon the earth, does not recognize the unnumbered blessings which he has enjoyed through this endeared relation?

His own infinite wisdom and boundless goodness prompted the Almighty Creator to ordain this beneficent relation, with all its sweet attractions and

20

happy endearments. Must he not, therefore, have made it honorable, noble, and dignified? And ought its elevation and importance to be forgotten and neglected? Surely it demands our most intelligent consideration and devout acknowledgment. But what mind has ever possessed a capacity enlarged and matured to comprehend fully the true dignity of a Mother?

Woman was formed by the glorious Creator as a "help-meet for man:" whatever dignity, therefore, attaches to him as a rational being, and the representative on earth of his Maker, is shared by the partner of his life, his other self. Woman is the equal participator of all the honors which pertain to human nature. But woman's highest dignity and her greatest honors are found in contributing to the perfection of the divine purpose of her Creator in her peculiar character of mother.

A mother's dignity, however, will but imperfectly appear unless she is considered as bringing into the world a rational offspring, whose existence will affect others, and will continue through eternal ages. Adam, by intuitive wisdom imparted from God, perceived this surpassing excellence when "he called his wife's name Eve," because she was the mother of all living, Gen. iii. 20. Woman must be contemplated as giving birth to those whose principles, characters, and labors will deeply and permanently influence individuals in the domestic circle, and which will be felt by large communities, and in some instances, at least, by the whole population of the world. Our blessed Lord acknowledges this sentiment, expressed by the woman respecting himself, when having seen his mighty works, and heard his wise discourses, she exclaimed, "Blessed is the womb that bare thee, and the paps which thou hast sucked."—Luke vi. 27. On this rational principle we cannot separate the greatness which distinguished the worthies of ancient and modern times, from the characters of their favored mothers. Watts, Doddridge, Wesley, King Edward, King Alfred, and many others, have immortalized their names by their personal virtues, and by their imperishable works to benefit their country; but while we contemplate and enjoy the fruits of their extraordinary labors, we cannot fail to reflect upon the influence of their excellent mothers. We cannot refrain from tendering to them the honor which is their due, on account of their noble endeavor to discharge their maternal obligations, rendering them public blessings.

Divine inspiration has directly sanctioned this principle in the case of the Virgin Mary. Congratulated by her venerable relative Elizabeth, mother by miracle of the herald prophet of Messiah, and filled with the Holy Spirit, who directed her to look forward to the future greatness of her mysterious Son, her enlightened and pious mind burst forth in devout admiration at the honor which would be ascribed to her on account of his unspeakable blessings to mankind. She gave expression to her elevated thoughts and said, "My soul doth magnify the Lord, and my spirit hath rejoiced in God my Saviour. For he hath regarded the lowliness of his hand-maiden.  For behold from henceforth, all generations shall call me blessed."— Luke i. 46–48.

Mothers in our time, though not dignified in the manner of the Blessed Virgin, and not warranted to anticipate a similar honor to that which attached to her name, may yet contemplate the influence which their children will have upon society, and their own honor will be secured and promoted by laboring to form their infant minds to religion, to virtue, and to love of their country.

Immortality especially gives dignity to its subjects : and hence arises, in no inconceivable degree, the exalted honor of a mother.   By the sovereign ordination of the Almighty, she gives birth, not to a being of a mere momentary existence, and whose life will perish as that of the beasts of the field, but to an immortal ! Her sucking infant, feeble and helpless as it may appear, possesses within its bosom a rational soul—an intellectual power—a spirit which all-devouring time cannot destroy,—which can never die—but which will outlive the splendors of the glorious sun, and the burning brilliancy of all the material host of heaven ! Throughout the infinite ages of eternity, when all these shall have answered the beneficent end of their creation, and shall have been blotted out from their positions in the immense regions of space, the soul of the humblest child will shine and improve before the eternal throne, being filled with holy delight and divine love, and ever active in the praises of its blessed Creator.

Likeness to the infinitely glorious Creator constitutes the chief dignity of our nature. And the intelligent, pious mother looks upon her infant offspring with adoring gratitude to God, as possessing that likeness. Originally, "the Lord God formed man of the dust of the ground, and breathed into his nostrils the breath of life, and man became a living soul."—Gen. ii. 7. By the same omnipotent and gracious will, God has given being to human souls through all generations as at the first creation; but the mother is honored as the medium of this mysterious creation in the case of every child. And though the moral likeness of its blessed Maker is defaced by the fall of our first parents, still, in thousands of instances, by means of early tuition and the prayers of the faithful mother, the child is "created in Christ Jesus in righteousness and true holiness."— Eph. ii. 10; iv. 24.

What, then, can be the greatness, dignity, and honor of her who is the appointed medium of such amazing powers and blessings! Must not mothers feel their high distinctions? Should they not frequently be invited to contemplate them? In this the security, the prosperity, and the happiness of our country, and even the welfare, the regeneration of the world, are involved; he, therefore, who is most successful in leading their minds to a proper, a rational and Scriptural view of this greatest of earthly relations, will most effectually engage, as he will most worthily merit, the gratitude and esteem of dignified, happy, and Christian mothers.

20*

## ON THE QUALIFICATIONS ESSENTIAL TO THE DISCHARGE OF MATERNAL DUTIES.

THE Rev. James Cameron, in his admirable lectures to mothers, observes:—

1. If you would train up your children in the way they should go, it is necessary that you *cultivate a deep and abiding sense of your own insufficiency.* I need say nothing, I am persuaded, to convince you of the fact of your insufficiency; if you have seriously reflected on the magnitude of your responsibility, you are ready to ask, "Who is sufficient for these things?" Your work is to train immortal beings for God—the same work, in substance, as that for which the Christian ministry has been instituted; and in reference to this work, even the Apostle of the Gentiles said, "We are not sufficient of ourselves to think anything as of ourselves."—2 Corinthians iii. 5. You are partakers of the same sinful nature with those whom you have to train, encompassed with all the weakness of fallen humanity, and subject to all its temptations. You have to contend against your own sinful propensities; to watch over your own spirits; to strive with your own waywardness; and in the midst of all this, to set before your children such an example of patience, forbearance, and holy living, as shall be a true and faithful comment on the sacred truths you teach them. If ever you become self-sufficient, be assured you will labor in vain; "for God resisteth the proud, but giveth grace to the humble."

But why do I urge upon you the consideration of your insufficiency? Is it to sink you into despair? Nay, verily; that were a profitless, as well as a cheerless undertaking. It is to induce you, in utter hopelessness of accomplishing the desired result by your own wisdom or strength, to cast yourselves on the God of all wisdom and of all strength, for it is written, "Cast thy burden upon the Lord and he will sustain thee." —Psalm lv. 22. "He giveth power to the faint, and to them that have no might, He increaseth strength. Even the youths shall faint and be weary, and the young men shall utterly fall; but they that *wait upon the Lord* shall renew their strength; they shall mount up with wings as eagles; they shall run and not be weary; and they shall walk and not faint."—Isaiah xl. 29, 31. You can have no fitness for your work, and no success in your work, but what comes from God. You cannot expect that God will grant this fitness and this success, unless you look to Him alone for them. But such is the natural unwillingness of the human heart to turn to God and to trust only in Him, that it is not till we are driven from every other refuge, and deprived of every other stay, that we cling to Him with the simple child-like dependence of those who have truly learned that there is no other God besides Jehovah; that all power, and all wisdom, and all blessings are from Him; and that without Him, every effort must be vain, and every undertaking abortive. The absolute helplessness and moral impotency of fallen man is one of the most important lessons we can be taught;

but alas! it is one of the most difficult for proud human nature to learn. The Spirit of God can teach it, and blessed are they who, being taught by the divine Spirit their own utter helplessness, are taught at the same time that they have a God to go to who can furnish them richly with all they need.

Again, then, I repeat, cultivate a sense of your insufficiency for the great work to which God has called you, and let this be so thoroughly interwoven in the very texture of your minds—let it so thoroughly pervade your whole habits of thinking and feeling, that you shall be kept in the very lowest depths of self-distrust, feeling that your only safety is in clinging, as with a death-grasp, to the soul-sustaining declaration, "My grace is sufficient for thee, for my strength is perfected in weakness."—2 Corinthians xii. 9. It is only when a deep sense of insufficiency, and a strong confidence in God are combined, that you are at all likely to be successful in your arduous work; your sense of insufficiency will make you cautious, tender, watchful, prayerful; and your confidence in God will nerve your soul, and strengthen you to grapple with the difficulties you have to encounter.

2. If you would train up your children in the way they should go, it is necessary that you *diligently cultivate your own minds, imbuing them with sound principles, and storing them with useful knowledge.* It may be said, that this ought to have been done before you occupied the position you do—and it is true. But it will be acknowledged, we think, by almost all who are

capable of forming a judgment on the subject, that generally speaking, it is not done before, and that in nine-tenths, perhaps, of those cases in which the mind has been fitted for the efficient discharge of a mother's duties, its cultivation has been chiefly, if not entirely effected, at a period subsequent to that allotted to what is termed *Education*. The education which females generally receive in youth, is but ill fitted for enabling them rightly " to mould the mass of human mind." Education properly so called is the training of the intellect, the conscience, and the affections. But is this a description of female education as it actually is, even with all the boasted improvements of modern times ? Is that education in any prominent degree, the education of the mind or heart at all, in any form ? Alas ! it is too frequently the cultivation of manner only. The useful is sacrificed to the ornamental. The casket is embellished with all kinds of tinsel-work, which may attract the admiration of the beholder, while the invaluable jewel it contains is left to comparative neglect. Let it not be supposed that we undervalue accomplishments. We believe them to be highly valuable—much more valuable than many who eagerly pursue them seem to be aware. But they may be too dearly purchased. And assuredly they are too dearly purchased, whenever they so engross the time and attention, as to leave little or no opportunity for the cultivation of the mind itself. It is distressing to think that while so much depends on the training of the female mind, so little provision is made for that training being effective. Napoléon once asked Madame Campan what the French nation most needed, in order that her youth might be properly educated. Her reply was comprised in one word—that word was—" Mothers !"    And it was a wise reply.   Not the French nation only—*the world* needs mothers, — Christian, intelligent, well-trained mothers, to whom the destinies of the rising generation may safely be entrusted.

A distinguished philosopher has remarked, that all the world is but the pupil and disciple of female influence ; how important, then, that females should be fitted for their work!   And is the education they generally receive in youth such as is likely to fit them for that work ?   No one acquainted with the subject will reply in the affirmative.   The end desired seems rather that they should be qualified for securing admiration and applause, than for moulding the minds and forming the characters of those who are to be the future defenders of the faith,—the ministers of the Gospel, the philosophers, the legislators, of the next generation.

I feel that I cannot do better than present you with the remarks of one of your own sex on this subject— one who is well entitled to an attentive hearing—I mean the author of " Woman's Mission :"

" What, then, is the true object of female education ? The best answer to this question is a statement of future duties; for it must never be forgotten, that if education be not a training for future duties, it is nothing.   The ordinary lot of woman is to marry.   Has

anything in these educations prepared her to make a
wise choice in marriage? To be a mother? Have
the duties of maternity—the nature of moral influence
—been pointed out to her? Has she ever been enlightened as to the consequent unspeakable importance
of personal character as the source of influence? In
a word, have any means, direct or indirect, prepared
her for her duties? No! But she is a linguist, a
pianist—graceful, admired. What is that to the purpose? The grand evil of such an education is the
mistaking means for ends: a common error, and the
source of half the moral confusion existing in the world.
It is the substitution of a part for the whole. The
time when young women enter upon life, is the one
point to which all plans of education tend, and at
which they all terminate; and to prepare them for
that point is the object of their training. Is it not
cruel to lay up for them a store of future wretchedness by an education which has no period in view but
one—a very short one, and the most unimportant and
irresponsible of the whole life? Who that had the
power of choice would choose to buy the admiration
of the world for a few short years with the happiness
of a whole life?

The temporary power to dazzle and to charm, with
the growing sense of duties undertaken only to be
neglected, and responsibilities, the existence of which
is discovered, perhaps simultaneously with that of an
utter inability to meet them. Even if the mischief
stopped here, it would be sufficiently great; but the

craving appetite for applause, once roused, is not so easily lulled again. The moral energies pampered by unwholesome nourishment—like the body when disordered by luxurious dainties, refuse to perform their healthy functions, and thus is sustained a perpetual strife and warfare of internal principles; the selfish principle still seeking the accustomed gratification, the conjugal and maternal prompting to the performance of duty; but duty is a cold word, and people, in order to find pleasure in duty, must have been trained to consider their duties as pleasures. This is a truth at which no one arrives by inspiration. And in this moral struggle, which, like all other struggles, produces lassitude and distaste of all things, the happiness of the individual is lost; her usefulness destroyed; her influence most pernicious. For nothing has so injurious an effect on temper and manners, and consequently on moral influence, as the want of that internal quiet, which can only arise from the accordance of duty with inclination.

I have a double object in view in directing your attention so prominently to this point—that you may bring these sentiments to bear on the education of your daughters; and that you may feel the necessity, whatever may have been the nature and extent of your own previous education, of continuing diligently to educate yourselves, and add to your resources. You will find that there is need of all, for you have a great work given you to do. Especially, let the sacred truths of God's Word be the subject of your constant study.

Be not content with a superficial knowledge of "the great things of God's law," but seek to know them in all their depth and fullness, tracing their bearings and connections, studying their harmonies and proportions; that thus, by having "the Word of Christ dwelling in you richly in all wisdom," you may be "thoroughly furnished unto all good works."

But though the Word of God must be your CHIEF study, beware of supposing it must be your only study. All truth is from God, and all truth may be made subservient to the great work of training your children for God. Indeed, if you confine your study to the Bible alone, you will not study to the best advantage; for, without the knowledge which is derived from other sources, a great part of the Bible will be to you a sealed book. All the knowledge we can acquire of whatever kind, and from whatever source, will, if rightly employed, aid us in our study of the Scriptures; and the wisdom of those who, decrying all kinds of secular knowledge, would limit us to the perusal of one book, even though that is God's own book, is of a piece with that of the fanatic who burned the Alexandrian library, and justified the act by pleading, that if these books contained nothing more than was taught in the Koran, they were unnecessary, and if they contained more, they were pernicious. Let the mind take an extensive range—as extensive as your time and circumstances will permit. If knowledge is power, then the more knowledge the more power. But mere power is not enough; unless combined with benevolence,

21

we have no security that it will be exercised for beneficial purposes. It may be employed to curse, not to bless—to destroy, not to save. Let all your knowledge, therefore, be baptized into Christ. Bring it to the foot of the Cross, and there let it be solemnly dedicated to the service of Him who died that sinful men might live. Thus shall you possess power combined with benevolence; for the religion of the cross is the religion of benevolence.

There is one department of knowledge which I would specially commend to your notice—I mean the knowledge of the mind itself. It is with mind you have to deal in training your children, and unless you are in some measure acquainted with the laws by which it is governed, and the manner in which it discharges its various functions, you will find yourself frequently at a loss; and more frequently still, you will fall into grievous blunders, without being aware of them, till the result shows that there has been something wrong, though you know not what. The musician, though utterly ignorant of the internal mechanism of his instrument, may elicit from it the most melodious sounds. He may thus operate successfully enough with the instrument; but he cannot operate successfully on the instrument. If it is out of tune, he cannot tune it; if it is impaired, he cannot repair it; he must have recourse to some one who understands its structure, and knows the laws which regulate the conveyance of sound. He can use the instrument, but he cannot (if we may be allowed such an expression) train the instrument. Even so—if your business were merely to operate by means of mind already formed, you might do much, though ignorant of the structure of mind—though even here you would feel the disadvantage of ignorance. But your business is to operate on mind itself—to adjust the instrument—to repair it when impaired—to tune it when out of tune.; and how is this to be done if you are ignorant of the principles of the mind which you have to train?

In all your conduct, manifest the most undeviating consistency. The adage, that example is more powerful than precept, is so trite, that you are in little danger of being allowed to forget it. But there is another truth which is more apt to be lost sight of—namely, that children, even at a very early age, are eagle-eyed to observe the inconsistencies of a parent; and the slightest inconsistency, though it be manifested only in a word or a look, lowers your influence over them in an inconceivable degree. When a child learns to distrust its mother, all her warnings, and admonitions, and remonstrances, however earnest and unremitting, fall powerless. This is the chief reason, it is to be feared, why we so frequently see the children of pious parents grow up impenitent.

The example of their parents has not been uniformly consistent with their instructions, and therefore have these instructions been useless. A writer in an American periodical relates the following incident, which may illustrate these remarks:

" A mother had a family of three interesting daughters, and requested me for a time to become their tutor. During the time I was thus employed, the pastor and an elder visited the house. The venerable minister affectionately inquired of the mother, if she was conscious of having faithfully discharged the duties of a Christian mother to her impenitent children? The mother replied, 'that she believed she had done all she could—she had prayed for them, and talked with them, until it seemed to do no good.' She professed great anxiety for them, and wished that they might be made the subjects of prayer. A few days after this visit, I called at my usual hour, and found that a lady of their acquaintance had stepped in for a fashionable call. She sat a few minutes, and was treated very civilly by Mrs. ——, and when she rose to leave, was very warmly urged to sit longer. She declined this, and as she left, Mrs. —— expressed the hope that they should have the pleasure of seeing her often. The hall door had scarcely closed, when the mother turned round in the presence of her daughters, and with a petulant air, 'wondered how people could find so much time to walk about the streets and trouble their neighbors.' Here, thought I, it is no difficult thing to see why 'it does no good' for the mother to 'talk about religion' to her daughters; and I thought it must be impious mockery for that mother to pray for the conversion of her children, while she continued to set before them such an example."

Mothers! watch your conduct. Your children watch it. Every expression of your countenance—

every word you utter—every action they see you perform, is scanned and scrutinized by them; and if they
perceive that you act inconsistently, they will in their
hearts despise you.   And you cannot long deceive a
child with regard to character; the only sure way to
appear consistent is to be so.

4.  Be firm and unbending in the exercise of your
authority, requiring on all occasions implicit, unresist-
ing obedience.   Implicit submission to the authority of
God is essential to true religion.   And God has given
you absolute authority over your child, that by being
habituated to the exercise of implicit submission to
your will, he may be trained to the exercise of implicit
submission to His.   Until your child is able in some
measure to judge for himself, you are to him in the
place of God; and if you allow your will to be disputed—if you shrink from the exercise of absolute, un-
compromising authority—you train your child to be a
rebel against God.   A mother's indulgence lays the
foundation for disobedience and insubordination toward
God; which, unless Divine grace in future years prevent, must issue in the child's eternal ruin.   And if
you would have your authority regarded, it must be
perfect.   If even once you allow it to be successfully
disputed, the consequences may be disastrous.   There
is no safety but in a uniform unbending decision, so
that your child may ever feel that there is but one
question with which he has to do, namely, "What does
my mother require?" and that when this is known, it
is utterly vain to think of questioning or disputing.
21*

This is a point of permanent importance. If you err here, you err fatally, and irrecoverably.

Let it not be said that the principle we inculcate is severe. It is not so. The most unbending authority may be blended with the most unwearied love. And the two ought ever to be blended. These are the two great principles of God's government, and your family government should resemble His. The unwearied exercise of love will prevent your authority from degenerating into harshness—the unbending exercise of authority will prevent your love from degenerating into foolish indulgence.

5. If you would train up your children in the way they should go, you must restrain and curb their wayward propensities. Never forget that they possess a depraved nature, prone to all evil,—averse from all good. Beware, therefore, of allowing them to have their own way. That is the way which leadeth to death. Accustom them by times to submit to restraint. Subject them to wholesome discipline; and do this in such a manner as shall prove even to themselves, that it is done not for the gratification of your passion, but for their profit. A child left to his own way will bring ruin on himself, and sorrow and disgrace on his parents. Remember the case of Adonijah. His father had not displeased him at any time in saying, "Why hast thou done so?" in other words, he was a spoiled child. And what was the consequence? His father's dying bed was disturbed by his treasonable machinations, and in order to secure the peace of the king-

dom, his own brother was obliged to issue an order for his death. Look at Eli. He was a good man, but a weak and irresolute parent. He allowed his sons to have their own way, until he had lost his authority over them, and when at length he remonstrated with them on the wickedness of their conduct, his words were unheeded : he was too late in beginning. And oh ! how dolefully must the message of the Lord by Samuel have fallen upon the old man's ears, and how must his heart have sunk within him when he listened to such words as these :—" I have told Eli that I will judge his house forever, for the iniquity which he knoweth ; because his sons made themselves vile, *and he restrained them not*. Therefore have I sworn unto the house of Eli, that the iniquity of Eli's house shall not be purged with sacrifice or offering forever."

6. It is of great importance that you begin the training of your children early. Perhaps one of the greatest mistakes into which mothers fall, is the mistake of supposing that the first two or three years of a child's life are unimportant as it regards his training. The truth is, that in reference to the formation of character, these years are the most important of all. From the impressions made, and the principles formed, during these years, your child's character for eternity may take its color and complexion. You cannot begin too early. Long before your child can speak, he is susceptible of moral training. We frequently hear mothers speak of their children being too young to be taught obedience, but no child is too young to be taught obe-

dience, who knows what he is expected to do, or from what he is expected to refrain; and the mother who acts on the maxim, that children may have their own way for a certain number of years, or even of months, will find, to her cost, that *that* lesson, at least, will not speedily be forgotten. When I speak of early training, I refer not to intellectual, but to moral training. Intellectual training is, perhaps, in the most of cases, commenced too soon, while the other and more important is neglected, though it is that of which an infant child is most capable.

Again, then, we repeat, begin early. Bend the twig while it is yet tender; not only is it then most easily bent, but it is most likely to retain the form you give it.

7. If you would train your children in the way they should go, you must make all their training bear, directly or indirectly, on their spiritual and eternal well-being. By this I do not mean that you should be always speaking to them *about* religion, for there is such a thing as forming in the mind of a child a permanent association between religious truth and the feeling of weariness or disgust; and against this evil, parents should especially guard. I mean that you should yourself always keep in view their eternal interests. It is not merely for the employment of the few fleeting years of the present life, that you are training them,—it is for the service and enjoyment of God forever. Oh, what a noble work is yours! Contemplate it in the light of eternity, and you will feel that it is the most dignified—the most glorious employment in which an

immortal being can engage. The thought that it is for eternity, will sustain you amidst every difficulty, and cheer you on in your noble career. Yes, it is a noble career! for when all the honor, and pomp, and glare of mere temporal pursuits have passed away, the effects of your work shall remain; and ceaseless ages shall record the triumph of your faith, and fortitude, and patience.

A celebrated painter was asked why he bestowed so much labor on all his productions? His answer was, "I paint for eternity." Christian mothers! in your case, this is literally true;—you train your children for eternity. Ought you not, then, to exercise unceasing care and vigilance?

8. It is surely scarcely necessary for me to add, as my last observation, that if you would train up your children in the way they should go, you must *abound in prayer*—fervent, wrestling, believing prayer. Without this, you can do nothing as it ought to be done. Great and arduous are your duties, and great is the preparation you need for the discharge of them. You need wisdom—you need firmness—you need decision—you need patience—you need self-control—you need perseverance—and whither can you go for these but to the mercy-seat of Him "who giveth unto all liberally, and upbraideth not?" "Every good gift and every perfect gift is from above, and cometh down from the Father of lights."—James i. 17. Continual prayer will fit you for your duties, and make these duties pleasant. By prayer you will lay hold on the strength

of God, and be able to say with the Apostle, "I can do all things through Christ, who strengtheneth me." —Philippians iv. 14.

I close these remarks by reminding you once more of the magnitude of your responsibility. To you (under God) are entrusted the destinies of the rising generation, and through it, the destinies of the generations following. The world looks to you; the Church of God looks to you; the spirits of departed saints look to you; the angelic hosts look to you; God himself looks to you—as those whose influence shall tell forever, on thousands yet unborn. Let a sense of the importance of your high calling animate you to run with patience the race that is set before you, and when you have finished your course, and are called to give in your account, yours will be the unspeakable happiness of being welcomed to the realms of glory by the approving voice of your Saviour God—"Well done, good and faithful servants, enter ye into the joy of your Lord." And with all your loved ones around you, you will stand on the Mount Zion when "earth and seas have fled," and with a heart overflowing with gratitude, will cast your crowns at Jesus' feet, saying, "Not unto us, not unto us, but unto Thy name be the glory."

---

## THE MOTHER'S CHARGE.

### BY W. B. SPRAGUE, D.D., ALBANY, NEW YORK.

LET me briefly illustrate *the nature of a mother's charge.* That charge is nothing less than a physical, rational, accountable, immortal, sinful, and social being.

It is a *physical* being. The babe that she embraces is a curious piece of the divine workmanship. Its little frame bears the stamp of infinite wisdom and goodness. It is exactly fitted to answer the purposes for which it is designed, is wanting in nothing, is superfluous in nothing. But yet it is only the germ of a man or a woman, destined, if it lives, to a natural process of expansion. That body is, indeed, nothing but finely-organized clay, and there does not essentially belong to it either the principle of immortality, or the principle of thought; but it is designed to be the organ of the soul's operations, and is to exert no unimportant influence upon the soul's character and destiny. If the body dies, the soul will still live; but if the faculties of the body are not suitably developed, the mind that inhabits it will find itself proportionably cramped, and contracted in its operations. Let no one say, "it matters not for the physical nature, if the higher nature be provided for," so long as the one is the medium through which the other acts. God hath joined them together in the economy of his creating wisdom; and man must have respect to the connection, as he would accomplish the end of his existence.

The mother's charge is a *rational* being. True, indeed, you see nothing in its earliest infancy to indicate that it possesses any higher faculties than the lamb, or the lark, or any other of the animal creation. But, helpless as it seems, unconscious as it seems, there is a glorious principle of intelligence belonging to it which time will ere long reveal, and which, if rightfully developed and directed, may render it a fit companion for an angel. Where all seems blank and dark, the light will ere long shine, and a mind that can discriminate, that can reason, that can feel, will be seen coming up in its strength and glory. Who knows but that it may be the mind of a Newton—who shall measure the heights and fathom the depths of the material creation? Who knows but that it may be the mind of a Locke, that shall bring out the mysteries of thought, and reveal to man the secret springs of his own conduct? Who knows but that it may be the mind of a Milton, attuned to heavenly melodies, and touched with a seraph's fire? What the particular character of her infant's mind is to be—whether of high degree or of low degree, the mother knows not—cannot know—enough that she knows that it is a spiritual, thinking, active principle, destined, by the decree of Heaven, to an indefinite expansion.

But to the power of thought is also joined the susceptibility of feeling; the infant is born with a *moral*, as well as a rational nature. In it are the elements of passions and affections, of desires and aversions, in which its happiness or unhappiness will chiefly be found, and which must decide, in a great degree, the complexion and destiny of the soul. Here, too, is concealed that noble principle of conscience, which, perhaps more than any other, bespeaks the dignity of human nature which is destined to occupy the judgment-seat in the soul, and to bring peace and joy, or remorse and terror, according to the decisions which it renders. In the earliest periods of infancy, there may be no higher happiness, or, at least, none apparent than freedom from bodily pain; and there may be no other suffering than what *consists* in bodily pain; but there is a hidden nature there susceptible of enjoyment or suffering, that outruns all human comprehension. There is that which may kindle into a consuming fire, and show itself great in wrath, in desolation, in self-torture; or which may glow with a genial fervor, diffusing serenity within, and shedding light and joy over the whole field of its influence.

And this leads me to say that the mother's charge is an *accountable* being. I do not mean to say, nor do I believe, that it is a moral agent from the beginning; nor would I venture to mark the point of intellectual development, when moral agency commences, believing, as I do, that that is one of the secret things which the Creator has retained in his own keeping;—I only mean, that, as the infant is constituted with a rational and moral nature, and is placed under the government of God, so accountableness is an essential attribute of that nature; and that before the accountableness can cease, the power of distinguishing and choosing between good and evil must cease. What a reflection to a mother, that the unconscious babe in her arms is constituted in such a way, that its actions shall ere long sustain a moral character; and that the whole history of its life shall be reviewed as a ground of approbation or of condemnation at the bar of the Eternal Judge!

The mother's charge, too, is *immortal*. The body will, indeed, last but a few short years ; now she folds it in her arms, and dandles it upon her knee ; but soon it will have expanded to the measure of a youth ; and at a period a little more distant, it will have reached its mature growth ; and a little later, if, indeed, it has not been earlier, it will return to the dust whence it came. But the spirit that gives the babe its chief interest, the soul that thinks, and speaks, and burns with celestial fire, is rendered imperishable, if not by the necessity of its nature, at least by its Creator's decree. The arms that enfold your babe will become clods, the sun that shines upon your babe will be extinguished, and the skies that attract its infant gaze will be rolled up as a burning vesture, and yet, all that is great and spiritual in that babe shall survive, not only in unimpaired, but constantly increasing energy. And for aught we know, other suns and worlds may take the place of these which we now behold, and, having fulfilled their end, may pass away as a midnight dream ; and others still may come up at the Creator's bidding to replenish immensity, and in obedience to a like decree, these may retire and be lost in the abyss of annihilation, and yet that infant mind, whose operations are now so feeble that you can scarcely detect them, will live through all this wreck of worlds, and even then will feel that its existence is only begun. When the Christian mother resigns her babe to the tomb in the budding season of its faculties, let her not look despairingly at the narrow house, as if her infant had perished there ; but let her rather think of the grave as the temporary dwelling-place of the corruptible, and be thankful that God has permitted her to make such a contribution to the immortal population of heaven.

The mother's charge is a *sinful* being. What! that smiling, unconscious babe, whose eyes have so lately been opened upon the light, a sinner! Not an actual transgressor of God's law—for of that we cannot suppose that its faculties render it capable—but a sinner in precisely the same sense that it is a rational being—there is that within it that will by-and-by kindle up and show itself a rational soul; and there is that within it also, that will by-and-by kindle and show itself a sinful disposition. I will not refer to God's Word now for the only satisfactory explanation of this fact; but the fact itself is proved by universal experience. Show me, if you can, an instance in the world's history, save that of the immaculate child Jesus, in which what has seemed innocent infancy did not prove itself the germ of sinning childhood. And, besides, if no hereditary stain have reached an infant's mind—in other words, if the infant be regarded as holy under the government of God, let us have the explanation of that bodily suffering under which it shrinks, and writhes, and sometimes even dies. Yes, mothers, talk as much as you will of your innocent babes, every one of them is the heir of an unholy nature, which will as certainly develop itself in unholy action, as that it develops itself at all. The new-born leopard may seem beautiful and harmless, and you fear not to take it up in your hands, or to press it to your bosom; but wait a while, and

you dare not look at it except some barrier intervene
to protect you; for it has shown itself possessed of a
nature the promptings of which would be to tear you
to pieces.   There was an infant born between thirty
and forty years ago that, doubtless, smiled upon its
mother with the same apparent innocence with which
other infants are wont to smile; and, possibly, some
advocate for the original purity of human nature may
have drawn an argument from what it seemed to be
in its helpless, unconscious state, to disprove that severe
creed which recognizes infants as inheriting a moral
taint from Adam; but that infant had not lived long
before he began to give proof that the orthodox creed
was sound.   In his boyhood he was revengeful and
wicked; in his manhood he was a murderer; and the
other day, when it was expected that the sun would
have gone down upon his body hanging in ignominy
between earth and heaven, it went down upon his body
self-bathed in his own blood.   Your children may not,
we trust will not, prove like *him;* but you deceive
yourselves if you imagine that, with all their loveliness,
they have not the same sinful nature which made him
a murderer.

The mother's charge has also a *social* nature.   As it
is not destined to exist in a state of solitude, so it is
endowed with a social propensity—with a disposition
to mingle with other beings, to whom it will impart
more or less of its own character.   No man lives for
himself alone.   As he is bound to society by various
ties, so every relation that he sustains is a channel of

influence for good or evil, that is operating constantly upon his fellow-men. It is a most serious thought that the infant in your arms, if it lives but a few years, will be an active member of society, and will not only be himself forming a character for eternity, but will be contributing an influence that will tell on the destinies of other minds through the whole period of their existence.

Such is the mother's charge; and where is the mother who can contemplate it without being ready to sink under the burden of responsibility which it imposes?

## A MOTHER'S PRIVILEGE.

"What is a mother's privilege? It is your privilege, Christian mother, and you must not neglect it, to train up your child for heaven. It is your privilege, Oh! ever prize it, to plead for him the promises of a covenant-keeping God. He bids you come: He will not suffer any one to forbid you, when with yearning soul you bear your little one, warmed in your bosom, its heart beating with kindred life against your own, to Him who died for you and your child. This is a mother's privilege, to win a blessing for the babe you love, that shall abide on its spirit through the eternity of its being. As it lies lapped in your guardianship, unconscious of the care that watches its slumbers, you can breathe over faith's heartfelt dedication of your love to your present God. As in gentlest ministry of tender-

22*

ness you open for it your bosom's fount, and give it as it were to drink from your own life, you can bear its name in all the urgency of a mother's love on your humble, holiest prayer! You can bind its soul around your own, inseparable from you, and never to be forgotten or neglected while life or hope is yours. To watch its infant passions, and check their promptings —to train its infant thoughts,—to twine around its infant heart a tie that Heaven will kindly own, and that shall wax stronger and stronger beneath a Saviour's smile,—this, this is a mother's privilege. Make it all your own. Think not it is enough to HOPE, but be sure to KNOW that your child is an heir of heaven. Promises bright with protection, and more precious still, with eternal life, beckon you on every page of God's revelation to labor for a world that needs salvation. Plead them—plead them mightily, and leave Him not till he bids you go in peace. Motives break forth in voices from heaven, bidding you 'Come in with thy child, come!' and in unearthly warnings from the pit, 'Turn him from every path that may bring him here;' and as they pour their tide of influence on your heart, they proclaim that you have a work of faith and labor of love to perform, in which you must not linger, nor faint, nor grow weary. Strengthen, then, that faith by feeding on the word of truth, and drink in, in communion with an all-sufficient Redeemer, the streams of life that may invigorate you to the noblest deed that your immortal spirit can accomplish. You must win that soul, instinct with dying energies, to be a living gem in the Saviour's crown. Pride would teach you to ask for greatness, for honors to laurel the brow of your loved one, for what the earth-born delight in and call happiness, to be his portion here; but ask for Him a greater boon than any or all of these; you must beg, and passing this narrow bound of time, your prayer must reach out to grasp a prize of which he can only know the worth, as he learns it where eternal ages stamp it never to be forgotten or unenjoyed. As if but one sole request, which must never be let go till it is granted, is your errand there, so make your urgency be felt at the footstool of the throne. A mother's voice—a mother's heart shall not plead in vain."

## MATERNAL PIETY.

" WHEN I say that there is a connection between the piety of mothers and the salvation of their children, I do not mean the connection which God has instituted in the covenant of grace; for this covenant applies equally to both parents. There is something peculiar in the case of a mother; so that, independently of the covenant of God, maternal piety is more likely to be followed by the conversion of children, than the piety of a father.

1st. This connection is very simple. *A mother's piety is peculiarly affectionate.* There is nothing severe or ceremonious in its exercise; but it mingles itself with the numberless little natural kindnesses by which the

heart of a child is won, and acquires a hold on the first
rising affections of his mind. A pious mother, while
she watches over her sleeping or sick child, while she
guides his tottering steps, or furnishes him for his
school, or his pastime, or leads him up to the house of
God, has a yearning of the soul over his soul, and
cherishes and often expresses a feeling of solicitude for
his eternal welfare, which diffuses a restraining and
chastening influence over his mind, while it is precious
also in the sight of God. Her prayers, which she pours
out over him, are in those wonted accents of tenderness
and love, which have always soothed his mind, and
kindled his affection. Her counsels, and admonitions,
and chastisements, are the manifest dictates of a heart
laboring with desires for his conversion and salvation,
and carry with them, on that account, an authority
which truth and reason alone would be unable to exert.

2d. *A mother's piety is familiar.* It labors with
her child, and before God in his behalf, in a style
which he understands and feels. The language of her
counsels and her devotions is a simple and artless expression of her desires adapted to his youth, his inex-
perience, his infirmities and temptations. It comes
home to his heart. He recognizes the voice that speaks
to him to be the same which has always lulled him
into his evening slumbers, and greeted him with morning salutations; and he feels that it means as much
kindness for him, when speaking in counsel, or in prayer, as when it has soothed his pains, or tempted his
smiles, or encouraged his festivities. If a father's

efforts for the spiritual good of his child produce more of reverence, solemnity, and fear; yet a mother applies herself more directly to the heart, and fastens there a cord, which holds the affections and the sensibilities, when the other more powerful emotions have subsided. A mother will teach her child, will soften, or restrain, or encourage him, with incomparably more facility and effect than any other individual. She will fix in his mind an outline of the whole history of the Bible, of its system of doctrines and precepts, sooner and better than any other person can initiate him into the first principles of Divine knowledge. He understands her tones, her looks, her gestures. They all speak to him, and they fix an impression which is always sure and abiding. And there is no time when a pious mother cannot have access to her child. How soon will she penetrate his heart, and ascertain the causes of all his troubles; how soon will she allay the storm of passion; how soon apply to him the admonitions of Providence; how soon excite an inquisitive spirit, and how successfully follow up a father's sterner reproof and correction, with heart-breaking expostulations, reducing him to penitence, and fortifying him against future temptation! A pious mother is a sort of better conscience to a child, a messenger of God ever the most ready and the most able, next to the Holy Spirit, to rescue him from the power of his depravity, and turn his feet into the paths of peace.

3d. *A pious mother has peculiar opportunities of saving her children.* She is ever at their side to restrain their corrupt propensities, to regulate their inordinate desires, and encourage them to obedience. She can turn almost every event of Providence into an occasion of salutary instruction, can mingle counsel as it were with their medicine and their food, can be ever distilling upon them the wholesome words of eternal life, as the dew upon the tender herb, and the soft rain that waters the earth. Her mind is not burdened with cares for their sustenance, but with anxieties for their salvation; and while preparing for them their raiment, while superintending their tasks or their sports, she can be lifting up to God her desires for their everlasting happiness. Her watchful eye can pierce through their duplicity, and search out their secret sins, while the leisure that God gives her for this very purpose can be employed in explaining to them the obligations and sanctions of the Divine law, the nature of their corruptions, the consequences of their sins, and the way of salvation, through the atoning sacrifice of Christ. It is hers to commend them to God, when she commits them to their pillows, and when she leads them out to the employment of the day. They may enjoy her guidance as their constant monitor, till they are qualified to go out to another residence; and her daily prayers and frequent correspondence may afterward keep alive the precious instructions of their childhood, and procure for them the better teaching and direction of the Holy Spirit. To the mother belongs most appropriately the duty and privilege of administering line upon line, and precept upon precept. To bring up her children for God is her great business, her honorable distinction, and it is connected in the Divine Providence with results the most encouraging and glorious. Not, indeed, that there is any intrinsic efficacy in the means which she employs, not that any means will *necessarily* procure the salvation of the soul; but so it is that God accomplishes the purposes of his mercy. He saves according to his pleasure; but he saves by instruments naturally fitted for his purpose. He sanctifies the mother's heart, that heirs of glory may be educated for his kingdom. He blesses her counsels and her prayers, because to this end He qualified her to promote the interests of his kingdom."

We cannot better conclude these forcible remarks than by the following affecting testimony and beautiful verses on the

### POWER OF MATERNAL PIETY.

"When I was a little child," said a good old man, "my mother used to bid me kneel down beside her, and place her hand upon my head while she prayed. Ere I was old enough to know her worth she died, and I was left too much to my own guidance. Like others, I was inclined to evil passions, but often felt myself checked, and as it were drawn back by a soft hand upon my head. When a young man, I traveled in foreign lands, and was exposed to many temptations; but when I would have yielded, *that same hand was upon my head*, and I was saved. I seemed to feel its pressure as in the days of my happy infancy, and sometimes there came with it a voice in my heart, a voice that must be obeyed—'O do not this wickedness, my son, nor sin against thy God.'"

### LINES ON THE ABOVE FACT.

"Why gaze ye on my hoary hairs,
    Ye children young and gay?
Your locks, beneath the blast of cares,
    Will bleach as white as they.

I had a mother once like you,
    Who o'er my pillow hung,
Kiss'd from my cheek the briny dew,
    And taught my faltering tongue.

She, when the nightly couch was spread,
    Would bow my infant knee,
And place her hand upon my head,
    And, kneeling, pray for me.

But, then, there came a fearful day!
    I sought my mother's bed,
Till harsh hands tore me thence away,
    And told me she was dead.

I plucked a fair white rose, and stole
    To lay it by her side;
And thought strange sleep enchained her soul,
    For no fond voice replied.

That eve I knelt me down in woe,
    And said a lonely prayer;
Yet still my temples seemed to glow
    As if that hand were there.

Years fled, and left me childhood's joy,
    Gay sports and pastimes dear;
I rose a wild and wayward boy,
    Who scorned the curb of fear.

Fierce passions shook me like a reed;
    Yet, ere at night I slept,
That soft hand made my bosom bleed,
    And down I fell, and wept.

Youth came—the props of virtue reel'd,
   And oft, at day's decline,
A marble touch my brow congealed—
   Bless'd mother,—was it thine?

In foreign lands I traveled wide,
   My pulse was bounding high;
Vice spread her meshes at my side,
   And pleasure lured my eye;—

Yet still *that hand*, so soft and cold,
   Maintained its mystic sway,
As when amid my curls of gold
   With gentle force it lay.

And with it breathed a voice of care,
   As from the lowly sod,
" My son—my only one—beware!
   Nor sin against thy God."

Ye think, perchance, that age hath stole
   My kindly warmth away,
And dimmed the tablet of the soul;—
   Yet when, with lordly sway,

This brow the plumed helm displayed,
   That guides the warrior's throng;
Or beauty's thrilling fingers strayed
   These manly locks among,

That hallowed touch was ne'er forgot!
   And now, though time hath set
His frosty seal upon my lot,
   These temples feel it yet.

And if I e'er in heaven appear,
   A mother's holy prayer,
A mother's hand and gentle tear,
That pointed to a Saviour dear,
   Have led the wanderer there."

23

## ON THE MOTHER'S DIFFICULTIES.

"It not unfrequently happens that a judicious and faithful mother is connected with a husband whose principles and example are anything but what she could desire. In such cases, not only does the whole government of the family devolve upon the mother, but the influence of the father is such, as, in a great degree, to counteract all her exertions. This is indeed a trying situation. It is, however, far from being a hopeless one. You must not give up in despair, but let the emergencies of the case rouse you to more constant watchfulness, and more persevering and vigorous effort. If a wife be judicious and consistent in her exertion, a father, in almost all cases, will soon find confidence in the management of the family, and will very gladly allow her to bear all the burden of taking care of the children. Such a father is almost necessarily much of the time absent from home ; and when at home, is not often in a mood to enjoy the society of his family. Let such a mother teach her children to be quiet and still when their father is present. Let her make every effort to accustom them to habits of industry. And let her do everything in her power to induce them to be respectful and affectionate to their father. This course is, indeed, the best which can be adopted to reclaim the unhappy parent. The more cheerful you can make home to him, the stronger are the inducements which are presented to draw him away from scenes into which he ought not to enter.

It is true, there is no situation more difficult than the one we are now describing. But that even these difficulties are not insurmountable, facts have not unfrequently proved. Many cases occur in which the mother triumphantly surmounts them all, and rears up a virtuous and happy family. Her husband is most brutally intemperate; and I need not here depict the scenes through which such a mother is called to pass. She sees, however, that the welfare of the family is dependent upon her, and accordingly nerves her heart resolutely to meet her responsibilities. She commences in the earliest infancy of her children, teaching them implicit obedience. She binds them to her with those ties from which they would never be able or desirous to break. The most abundant success rewards her efforts. The older her children grow, the more respectful and attentive they become, for the more clearly they see that they are indebted to their mother for salvation from their father's disgrace and woe. Every sorrow of such a mother is alleviated by the sympathy and affection of her sons. She looks around upon them with feelings of maternal gratification, which no language can describe. They feel the worth and dignity of her character. Though her situation in life may be humble, and though her mind may not be stored with knowledge, yet her moral worth, and her judicious government, command their reverence.

In a family of this sort, in one of the States of Ameri-

ca, one cold December night, the mother was sitting
alone by the fire, between the hours of nine and ten,
waiting for the return of her absent husband. Her
sons, fatigued with the labors of the day, had all retired to rest. A little before ten, her husband came
in from the neighboring store, where he had passed the
evening with his degraded associates. He insisted in
calling up the boys at that unseasonable hour, to send
them into the wood-lot for a load of wood. Though
there was an ample supply of fuel at the house, he
would not listen to reason, but stamped and swore that
the boys should go. The mother, finding it utterly in
vain to oppose his wishes, called her sons, and told
them that their father insisted upon their going with
the team to the wood-lot. She spoke to them kindly ;
told them she was sorry they must go ; but, said she,
'Remember that he is your father.' Her sons were
full-grown young men. But at their mother's voice,
they immediately arose, and without a murmur, brought
out the oxen and went to the woods. They had perfect confidence in her judgment and her management.
While they were absent, their mother was busy in preparing an inviting supper for them on their return.
The drunken father soon retired. About midnight,
the sons finished their tasks, and entering the house,
found their mother ready to receive them with cheerfulness and smiles. A bright fire was blazing upon
the hearth. The room was warm and pleasant. With
keen appetites and that cheerfulness of spirits which
generally accompanies the performance of duty, those

children sat down with their much-loved parent to the repast she had provided, and soon after, all were reposing in the quietude of sleep.

Many a mother has been the guardian and saviour of her family. She has brought up her sons to industry, and her daughters to virtue. And in her old age, she has reaped a rich reward for all her toil, in the affections and attentions of her grateful children. She has struggled in tears and discouragement for many weary years, till at last God has dispelled all the gloom, and filled her heart with joy in witnessing the blessed results of her fidelity. Be not, therefore, desponding. That which has once been done, may be done again."

---

## METHOD OF IMPARTING SCRIPTURAL KNOWLEDGE.

### BY REV. J. ABBOTT.

It is of great consequence that you pursue a proper course in endeavoring to interest your children in the study of the Scriptures. Upon a proper use of this volume everything depends. There are some parts which children can at a very early age understand and appreciate. Others, from their style and subject, will act efficiently on mature minds alone. From the former, which ought to be early read and explained, an important and most immediate religious influence can at once be expected. Selections from the latter should be fixed in the memory, to exert an influence in future years.

23*

For the former of these purposes, the *narrative parts*, if judiciously selected, are most appropriate in early years. But great care ought to be taken to select those which may be easily understood, and those to which some moral lesson is obvious and simple. Let it be constantly borne in mind that the object in view in teaching the Bible to a child, is to *affect his heart ;* and it would be well for every mother to pause occasionally, and ask herself, "What moral duty am I endeavoring to inculcate now ?" "What practical effect upon the heart and conduct of my child is this lesson intended to produce ?" To ask a young child such a question as, "Who was the first man ? Who was the oldest man ? Who slew Goliath ?" may be giving him lessons in pronunciation, but it is not giving him *religious instruction*. It may be to teach him to articulate, or it may strengthen his memory; but it is doing little or nothing to promote his piety. I would not be understood to condemn such questions, I only wish that parents may understand their true nature. If the real or supposed dexterity of the child in answering them is not made the occasion of showing him off before company, thus cherishing vanity and self-conceit, it may be well thus to exercise the memory; and some facts, which will be useful hereafter, may be fixed in this way. But it must not be considered as religious instruction; it has not in any degree the *nature* of religious instruction.

What, then, is the kind of instruction which is to be given from the Bible? I will illustrate the method by supposing a case which may bring the proper principles to view. We will imagine the child to be three or four years old.

"Come," says its mother, "come to me, and I will read you a story." It is Sabbath afternoon, we will suppose; the mind of the child is not preoccupied with any other interest. "Sometimes," continues the mother, "I tell you stories to amuse you; but I am not going to do that now, it is to do you good. Do you understand how it will do you good to hear a story?"

"No, mother."

"Well, you will see. It is the story of Cain and Abel. Do you know anything about it?"

"Yes, Cain killed Abel."

"Do you know why he killed him?"

"Because he was wicked."

"No, I mean what did Abel do to make Cain angry with him? Did you ever see anybody angry? Were you ever angry yourself?"

"Yes, mother."

"And I suppose you had some cause for it? Now I will read the account, and see whether you can tell me what made Cain angry. '*And Cain brought of the fruit of the ground an offering unto the Lord.*' Do you know what the fruit of the ground is?"

"No, mother."

"It means anything which grows out of the ground. Cain was a farmer : he planted seeds and gathered the fruits which grew from them, and he brought some of them to offer them to God. '*And Abel brought of the firstlings of his flock.'* Do you know what that means ?"

The child hesitates.

"Abel did not cultivate the ground like Cain. He had great flocks of sheep and goats, and he brought some of the best of those to offer to God. So that you see that Cain and Abel did almost exactly the same thing.

"Now God does not notice merely *what we do, but how we feel while we* are doing it. If I should ask you to go and shut the door when you are busy, and if you should go immediately, but feel ill-humored, God would be displeased. He looks at the heart. Do you ever feel ill-humored, when I wish you to do what you dislike ?"

"Yes, sometimes."

"Now Cain, I suppose, did not feel pleasantly when he brought his offering, and God was dissatisfied with him. But God was pleased with Abel's offering, and accepted it. Should you have thought that Cain would have liked this ?"

"No,—did he like it ?"

"No, he did not; and it is very remarkable that he was displeased not only against God, but he was angry with his brother, who had not done him the least wrong. That is the way with us all. If you should do wrong, and sister do right, and I should blame YOU and praise HER, you would be tempted to feel angry with her, just because she had been so happy as to do her duty. How wicked such a feeling is !

" Cain, however, had that feeling, and little children have it very often. It shows itself in different ways. Cain being a strong man, rose against his brother in the field, and killed him. But young children who are weak and small, would only strike each other, or say unkind things to one another. Now, God is displeased with us when we have these feelings, whether we show them by unkind words, or by cruel actions. There is a particular verse in the Bible that shows this. Should you like to have me find it ?"

" Yes, mother."

" I will find it, then. It is in Matthew v., 22 ; our Saviour says it. It is this, ' Whosoever is angry with his brother without a cause, shall be in danger of the judgment ; and whosoever shall say, Thou fool, shall be in danger of hell-fire.' This is not the whole verse. I will explain the other part some other time."

The reader will observe at once, that the kind of instruction here exemplified, consists in drawing out the moral lesson which the passage is intended to teach, and in giving it *direct* and *practical application*, to the circumstances and temptations of the child.

---

## LET EVERY MOTHER LOOK TO THE CHRISTIAN EDUCATION OF HER OWN CHILD.

"THE professed followers of Christ receive the Word of God as the only rule of life, and do, in some important cases, so modify their interpretations of it, by the customs and maxims of a world lying in wickedness, that they actually follow the dictates of a depraved heart. Their confidence is placed, partly in their own worldly wisdom, and partly in the power and faithfulness of God.

It is to be feared that the Bible system of education is strangely perverted by worldly wisdom. 'Train up a child in the way he should go, and when he is old he will not depart from it.'

The family circle was appointed by Infinite Wisdom, as a nursery of all those principles which assimilate man to his Creator. How should we ever be able to form any adequate conception of our Father who is in heaven, or of the endearing relation in which we stand to Him, if we had never known the bond which unites the earthly parent and child?

Let a child be properly taught his duty to his earthly parent, that he may comprehend the higher one which he owes to 'our Father in heaven.'

The religious instruction of children, given by the parents in the family, enforced by a consistent example, and accompanied with fervent prayer, furnishes fathers and mothers with the only well-grounded hope that their children will be prepared to meet the temptations of the world.

How exalted the privilege, and how lofty the destiny of the rising generation! and how momentous the responsibilities resting upon Christian parents! Christian mothers, weigh well the truth, that the most solemn obligations are pressing upon you to attend personally, faithfully, and prayerfully, to the religious education of your children. If you would save your child from infidelity, trust not the moulding of his young mind to unhallowed hands. A child acquires a perfect confidence in its mother: hence her influence is greater than any other.

Who can so well discover the unfolding intellect of a child as the mother? Who can so well apply seasonable instruction as the watchful mother?

The first impressions are fixed principles, and your example may make them either good or bad. Children are ever watching for something new from their mother, and, through the corrupt propensities of human nature, they will be far more ready to catch the evil than the good. How important, then, that your every act be consistent and correct, that the first impressions made upon the mind of your child be salutary!

Christian mother, consider how far your own conduct will tell upon the future weal or woe of your child's soul in eternity. By your apathy and negligence your child may be lost; by your prayerful, persevering watchfulness, care, and instruction, through Christ, your child may be saved.

'Let your grand object be, to make your child, while yet a child, a believer in the Bible.' Thoroughly explain to him its doctrines, precepts, and promises. Teach him the theory of the Gospel, prayerfully submitting the whole to God, *believing* the Holy Spirit will do his office-work upon the heart. But above all, beware how you encourage your child to hope his little heart is regenerated, merely because he has learned and knows it to be necessary. Close discrimination is necessary, that *you* do not deceive your child, and lead him to believe his heart is changed, when in fact it is not. Rest not satisfied until the fruits of the Spirit are manifested by the works of repentance and faith. Even little children may be converted; and when you are satisfied, by scriptural evidence, of the conversion of your child, be not satisfied with yourself, and think your work is done. It remains your duty, and your privilege, by the grace of God assisting you, to guide his young feet in the footsteps of our Saviour, the pathway to God, and eternal life. Mother, is it of small moment that you have in solemn charge the disposal of 'intelligence and immortality,' on which hangs the issue of eternity? Does not your heart respond to this awful responsibility? Then ever be found with a prayerful spirit, which is a 'Mother's panoply.' Pray without ceasing."

---

### INFANT EDUCATOIN.

"FIRST. A watchful observance and management of the temper, the abuse of which is the impulse to violence and anger, should commence when the child first opens its eyes upon its mother's countenance. The utmost that can then be attempted, is the diversion of the infant from the feeling, when excited, and from its object, and the avoidance of all exciting causes. If this be neglected, a bias is given, which it is difficult ever afterward to correct.

Second. The child so managed by his nurse as to escape the first trials of temper, should be introduced as early as possible to his fellows of the same age; the best time is when he begins to walk, for it is chiefly in the society of his fellows that the means of his moral training are to be found.

Third. It is advantageous, perhaps necessary, that his fellows should be moderately numerous, presenting a variety of dispositions—an actual world into which he is introduced—a world of infant business and intercourse—a miniature—and it is so of the adult world itself. Such is the infant school when well conducted.

Fourth. But this intercourse must not be at random. It must be correctly systematized, and narrowly superintended and watched, by well-instructed and habitually moral persons.

Fifth. The mother's own relation to the infant charge should be marked by affection, cheerfulness, mirth, and that activity of invention which delights and keeps alive the infant faculties.

Sixth. The infants should be permitted to play together out of doors, in unrestrained freedom; a watchful eye being all the while kept upon the nature and manner of their intercourse.

Seventh. Unceasing encouragement should be given to the practice of generosity, gentleness, mercy, kindness, honesty, truth, and cleanliness in personal habits;

24

and all occasions of quarrel, or cruelty, or fraud, or falsehood, should be minutely and patiently examined into, and the moral balance, when overset, restored; while, on the other hand, all indelicacy, filthiness, rudeness, covetousness, unfairness, dishonesty, violence, cruelty, insolence, vanity, cowardice, and obstinacy, should be repressed by all the moral police of this infant community. No instance should ever be passed over.

Eighth. There ought to be much well-regulated muscular exercise in the play of the infants, which should be as much as possible in the open air.

Ninth. Their school-hall and nursery should be large, and regularly ventilated when they are out of it, and when they are in it, if the weather permits; and the importance of ventilation, air, exercise, and cleanliness, should be unceasingly illustrated and impressed upon them as a habit and a duty.

Tenth. Every means of early implanting taste and refinement should be employed; for these are good pre-occupants of the soil, to the exclusion of the coarseness of vice.

The play-ground should be neatly laid out with borders for flowers, shrubs, and fruit-trees, tasteful ornaments erected, such as statues, founts, and the like, which the coarse-minded are so prone to destroy, and the infants habituated not only to respect, but to admire and delight in them; while the entire absence of guard or restraint will give them the feeling that they are confided in, and exercise yet higher feelings than taste and refinement.

Eleventh. The too prevalent cruelty of the young to animals often from mere thoughtlessness, may be prevented by many lessons on the subject, and by cherishing the actual habit of kindness to pets kept for the purpose, such as a dog, a cat, rabbits, ducks, &c., and by permitting them to hear all cruelty, even to reptiles, reprobated by their teacher and by their companions. An insect or reptile, not poisonous, ought never to be permitted to be killed or tortured. The habit acquired by brothers of teasing their sisters should never be tolerated.

Twelfth. The practice of teasing idiots or imbecile persons in families, or in the streets, ought to be held in due reprobation, as ungenerous and cruel. In the same way, other hurtful practices, even those which are the vices of men advanced in years, may be prevented by anticipation.

For example, ardent spirits-drinking may, for the three or four years of infant training, be so constantly reprobated in precepts, illustrative stories of the mother or teacher, and the ready acquiescence of the whole establishment, as to be early and indissolubly associated with poison and crime; instead of being, as is now too much the case, held up to the young as the joy and privilege of mankind.

Thirteenth. Many prejudices, fears, and superstitions which render the great mass of the people intractable, may be prevented from taking root by three or four years' contrary impressions; superstitious terrors, the supernatural agencies, and apparition of witches and ghosts, distrust of the benevolent advances of the richer classes, suspicious envyings, absurd self-sufficiencies and vanities, and many other hurtful and anti-social habits of feeling, may be absolutely excluded, and a capacity of much higher moral principle established in their stead."

---

## ON THE EDUCATION OF DAUGHTERS FOR USEFULNESS BOTH AT HOME AND ABROAD.

" It has often of late been to me an interesting inquiry, why so few of our daughters are prepared for missionary life; why, when a young missionary looks around upon the society in which he is accustomed to mingle, for a suitable companion to accompany him as the partner of his joys and sorrows to far-distant lands, is he compelled so often to search through the length and breadth of the land before he can find one qualified and willing to join him in his labor of love? I appeal to mothers for answers to these queries—to mothers to whom are committed the training of the heart and mind for the service of the Saviour.

I have thought the answer might be found in the fact that there is, at the present day, a great mistake pervading the minds of the community on this subject. Is not the opinion too prevalent that a *high standard of excellence* is not required for the performance of the common duties of life?

Christian mothers are educating two classes of Christian daughters. By far the larger class are preparing for usefulness, it is to be hoped—but for usefulness *at home.* While here and there a solitary daughter of Zion consecrates herself to missionary work, and we look upon her almost as the being of another world; and her education is carefully directed, and those habits are formed which will best prepare her for the situation she is about to fill.

Now suppose each pious mother, 'as a new bud of immortality blooms' within her dwelling, accepts the gift with the feeling that this loved treasure is to be cultivated for God; is to be trained for missionary life; is to develop that character which shall fit her for the quiet duties of domestic life, and that active benevolence which will make her a ministering angel in the abodes of poverty and degradation; that she is to be educated for *any situation* which God in his holy providence may call her to fill.

Let mothers cultivate the feeling that their beloved children are committed to them in trust, to be prepared to become co-workers with the Redeemer in extending the triumphs of his cross through the earth, and we should not see so many shrinking from the sacrifice when called upon to relinquish their loved ones for this blessed work. Said a mother who professes to love the service of her Lord, to one entrusted with the education of her daughters, 'Do all you can to bring my children in Christ's family, but you must not induce them to become missionaries.' Does not this language, *existing in the heart* of many a Christian mother,

24*

strikingly illustrate the truth of my remark, that two classes of female disciples are educating in the church? And does not the fact that so many of our daughters, when urged to think of their personal interest in the subject, meet you with the remark, ' We have not the qualifications for missionary life; *we are only fit to remain at home,*' most convincingly point us to this great mistake as the cause of this low standard of Christian feeling and duty?

The truth is, while we agree to pray, that the *angel* having the everlasting Gospel to preach unto them who dwell on the earth *may speed his flight,* we, who are training the generation that are to be the great instruments in the world's conversion to Christianity, forget, or seem to forget, that to effect this, ' our sons should be as plants *grown up in their youth;* our daughters *as corner-stones polished after the similitude of a palace;*' and that they must be educated with the sentiment, written as with a sunbeam on their hearts, ' Ye are not your own—ye are bought with a price; therefore glorify God in your body and in your spirits, which are God's.' It may be that our children shall never be called to the duties and trials of missionary life, but thus educated, they *will be prepared,* whatever their stations in life may be, or however solemn the responsibilities which may cluster around them, to scatter life and salvation in the pathway of many a wanderer—to lighten the burden of many a weary soul; and when their course on earth is ended, and they are called to join in the triumphant song of praise in heaven, the blessing of many comforted, strengthened, and assisted by their Christian counsels and efforts, will follow them to the throne of *God*."

---

### EARLY RELIGIOUS IMPRESSIONS, THE APPROPRIATE WORK OF MOTHERS.

" The subject of parental responsibility, which has formerly been so imperfectly appreciated, and still more imperfectly practiced, is, at the present day, frequently and powerfully presented for consideration. Yet there is no danger of exhausting the subject. To reflecting minds, and especially those of parents, it must rise in importance in proportion as it is dwelt upon.

No parents, then, need hesitate in bringing forward the fruits of their observation and experience. Although I have read much, thought much, and heard much; yet the subject now presents itself with the firmness and force of a new idea, particularly on the point of *maternal* responsibility. When I look at it, it seems as if the character, the present and eternal welfare of the rising generation, were placed almost exclusively and unqualifiedly in the hands of mothers. This conviction is not the result of abstract reflection, but of actual observation. God has, indeed, been pleased to recover to himself some who have not been brought to him in his appointed way. With regard to those who, we have reason to fear, have been lost, and to those who we now see in the broad way to destruction, we may challenge the scrutiny of an accurate inquirer; and we would not fear for the ground which we take, that among that unhappy number, few will be found who were blest with *judicious, pious, praying mothers,* who had the training of the first years of their children's life.

In reply to this, it may be said, we have known or heard of many of the children of pious parents who have lived and died irreligious. But if these cases were to be individually and faithfully investigated, a very different impression would remain on the mind. Among those who are nominal professors, how many realize as they ought their duties and responsibilities? Sometimes these examples, which are held up to disprove the argument, may have been the children of a pious father, but not of a pious mother; or the mother may have become pious after the children had passed that early and impressible period, within which the rudiments of the character are formed. And there are also pious parents who have not suitably estimated or fulfilled these duties, and so far have committed sin.

Again, there are some who have appeared, in their childhood, to have enjoyed faithful religious instruction, and pious prayers and example, and yet have been among those who are wandering far from God, and throwing off all the restraint of education and conscience. But if you will observe their course, you will find that among the converted and recovered wanderers, those who have had these advantages form much the greater proportion.

I am led to trace the history of such an individual. Little E. had the misfortune of losing his excellent mother before he reached his sixth year. Although, during his infantile years, her health had been so imperfect as to interfere with the discharge of her maternal duties, yet she had offered her children in faith to God. She had aimed to instill into their minds, on the first dawning of reason, a sense of their obligations and duties to their Creator, of whom she spoke to them as their Heavenly Father — their kind Preserver, and bountiful Benefactor. She cultivated sentiments of devotion by storing their minds with forms of prayer, and instructive hymns suited to their comprehension. And these instructions seemed to fall on good ground, and promised to bring forth fruit; and were not only thus implanted, but were watered with importunate prayers and tears. It pleased God, whose ways to us are inscrutable, to bereave this child of this precious blessing; and he was left, as it were, at the mercy of a wicked world, or as a helpless lamb without a shepherd. Little E. was left very much to the society and baneful example and influence of unprincipled servants. Soon all the gentle admonitions and pious instructions of his mother were effaced from his volatile mind. His conscience, which was once alive and tender, was soon seared; and when he was led into evil, he had no compunctions. As might be expected, as he advanced in years, he advanced in sin, from wanton indulgence, unchecked and unrestrained. As he progressed toward manhood, snares thickened around him, and he was thrown among evil companions. He advanced from one stage of wickedness to another, and still another, with fearful strides. The cavilers enjoyed the triumph of saying, 'There is the child of a pious mother.' They may enjoy this triumph. But in after years, if they beheld this youth in his headlong career arrested—if they could see the tears of contrition which he was brought to shed, and hear him recall his early impressions received from the lips of his tender mother, especially her dying advice, which, amidst all his wanderings, would sometimes recur—would they not yield their prejudices, and acknowledge that early impressions may radically affect the character and destiny of man?"

## A MOTHER'S LOVE.

BY MISS CATHERINE H. WATERMAN.

### I.

A MOTHER's love ! the fadeless light
    That glimmers o'er our weary way ;
A star amid the clouds of night,
    An ever-burning, quenchless ray.
A guarding power, thro' good and ill,
    Where'er the truant footsteps rôve ;
A ceaseless, flowing, sparkling rill,
    A fount of hope—a mother's love.

A mother's love—it whispers first
    Above the cradled infant's head,
And when those human blossoms burst,
    Her bosom's still the flowret's bed.

When their bright summer day has past,
    And autumn clouds hang dark above,
It lingers round us to the last,
    That dearest boon—a mother's love.

And yet how oft our footsteps roam,
    Through pleasure's bright, alluring maze,
Forgetful of the ties of home,
    And all the joys of earlier days!
But there's a charm to lure them back,
    And like the weary, wandering dove,
The heart re-wings its childhood's track,
    To that one ark, a mother's love.


### II.

" O, tell me not of maiden's love,
    That earth nor time can sever,
That deep within some gentle heart
    Burns brightly and for ever.

Nor yet of manhood's changeless faith,
    That first in youth was plighted,
Which ne'er is dimmed by care or age,
    And ne'er by coldness blighted.

These have their charms, but well I know
    The heart that feels no sorrow,
May by misfortune's withering blow
    Be broken ere to-morrow.

And well I know by cold neglect
    The fairest flower will languish;
And unkind looks from those we love,
    Oft rend the heart with anguish.

But there's a pure and holy flame,
    That coldness ne'er can smother;
And there's a charm of sacred power
    Dwells in the name of MOTHER!

Nay, though all other friends depart,
  E'en those we loved and cherished,
She twines around the drooping heart,
  Till its last bright hope hath perished.

She who hath watched the cradle-bed
  Where infancy is lying,
Gently she soothes the aching head,
  When that same form is dying.

O, think thou not that ties like these
  Death's icy touch can sever ;
Though sorrow dims the spirit's glow,
  True love shall last for ever."—ANON.

### III.

" Oh ! in our sterner manhood, when no ray
Of earlier sunshine glimmers on our way ;
When girt with sin and sorrow, and the toil
Of cares, which tear the bosom that they soil ;
Oh ! if there be in restrospection's chain
One link that knits us with young dreams again—
One thought so sweet, we scarcely dare to muse
On all the hoarded raptures it reviews ;
Which seems each instant, in its backward range,
The heart to soften and its ties to change,
And every spring untouched for years to move,
It is—THE MEMORY OF A MOTHER'S LOVE !"—H.

**THE END.**